CW01521886

The Flat Owners Guide

By Paul Walentowicz

With a foreword by Russell Campbell

Shelter

ACKNOWLEDGMENTS

This book is an extensively revised and updated edition of the title first published in 1988 and revised in 1995. Since then, important additional rights for flat owners have been introduced by the 1996 Housing Act. The opportunity has also been taken to include a new chapter on leaseholder management companies, a new section giving advice to owners with financial problems, lists of useful addresses and publications and an index.

In preparing this book I gratefully acknowledge the advice and assistance of Russell Campbell, Shelter's solicitor, and Imogen Wilson, head of publishing at Shelter. Thanks are also due to Linda Davies for her valuable editorial guidance.

Paul Walentowicz
September 2000

ISBN 1 870767 829

Published by:
Shelter
88 Old Street
London
EC1V 9HU
020 7505 2000
Registered Company 1038133
Registered Charity 263710

Production:
Davies Communications
020 7482 8844

Contents

Foreword

BY RUSSELL CAMPBELL
SOLICITOR, SHELTER

This is the third edition of the *Flat Owners Guide* originally published by SHAC in 1988. The last edition was also written by Paul Walentowicz and was published in October 1995. At the time, the book was recognised as providing a wealth of information about flat ownership, a phenomenon which had become increasingly common and increasingly complicated since the wholesale conversion of large properties in cities into flats in the 1950s and 1960s.

Over time, alongside weekly and monthly tenants there grew up a category of new owner, holding long leases (and, in many cases, displacing the former periodic tenants). Although these leases undoubtedly feel very different to both freeholder and lessee than any weekly or monthly tenancy, both interests are built upon the same foundation of landlord and tenant law. As a result, long lessees continue to find that they encounter difficulties not anticipated when they embark on 'ownership' of their flats. Government soon recognised the seriousness of these problems and in due course a series of statutes, including the Landlord and Tenant Act 1987 and the Leasehold Reform, Housing and Urban Development Act 1993, improved the position for flat owners. The process of reform is far from complete, with the Leasehold Reform and Commonhold Bill offering flat owners the opportunity to end their relationship with landlords altogether.

Paul Walentowicz's new edition of the *Flat Owners Guide* provides an excellent route through the maze of common law and statutory provisions and leads the reader to a place where the possibilities of an altogether new world become visible!

Although not a legal textbook or technical manual, the guide will prove extremely useful to flat owners in England and Wales, whether they are contemplating moving into ownership or they need advice on the best way to deal with problems. Paul's lucid style and practical approach are exactly what is needed to help flat owners express the rights they have. Flat owning will never be completely problem-free but in this guide flat owners have a trusty ally to help them on their way.

At the time of going to press it has been announced that the Leasehold Reform and Commonhold Bill will be included in the Queen's Speech on 6th December 2000. The prospects for further radical reform are good.

Introduction

Over recent years, flat ownership has become increasingly common. In many areas house prices have grown to such a level that many people, and especially first time buyers, can only afford to buy a flat. In London, in particular, on the one hand there is a shortage of moderately sized houses suitable for the smaller modern household but on the other hand a large stock of older, bigger properties suitable for conversion into flats. And in London and a few other big cities, there is still a residue of large, old mansion blocks of flats, many of which are now sold on long leases rather than let short-term. In many inner urban areas and in many parts of the South and South-East of England property prices are so high or space is so tight that often builders can only erect a block or blocks of flats on their new developments. In addition, there are now a sizeable number of households who occupy flats, most often purchased under the right to buy legislation, which are in blocks owned by local authorities.

Flat statistics

Just over one million households or about two million men, women and children – 8 per cent of all owners – own a flat in England. About half of these privately owned flats are in London. One quarter of flat owners also own part or all of the freehold. Four out of five flat owners have at least 80 years to run on their current lease. Flat owners are most common in London – 28 per cent of all home owners – and in the South of England – 13 per cent of all home owners. They are least common in the East Midlands – 1 per cent of all home owners – and in Yorkshire and Humberside – 2 per cent of all home owners. There are, unfortunately, no similar statistics about flat ownership in Wales.

Many people who are buying or have bought a flat simply regard themselves as home owners just like their neighbours or friends who live in houses. But, in fact and in law, they are actually tenants with long residential leases. They do, of course, have many more rights and obligations, such as to pay for repairs, than do ordinary tenants with short leases. In effect, flat owners purchase the temporary ownership of the flat subject to a diverse range of conditions and responsibilities. The landlord retains many rights and responsibilities, such to carry out timely repairs, over the building in which the flat is situated.

Long residential leases

The long residential lease is essentially a British phenomenon. In virtually every other country, including Scotland, you either buy a property or you rent a property. Flats in England and Wales are sold leasehold because most lawyers consider it inappropriate, and fraught with legal complexity, to create a freehold interest of just part of a building. As a result it is very rare to come across a flat which is owned freehold.

The basis of the landlord and flat owner relationship is the lease. Leases are complex documents which state precisely, although in legal jargon, the terms upon which the sale of the flat is made. These terms are binding on both the landlord and flat owner. In addition to the lease, further rights and responsibilities affecting the landlord and flat owner are found in legislation passed by Parliament and in the decisions of the courts.

Several recent Acts of Parliament, most notably, the 1987 Landlord and Tenant Act; the 1993 Leasehold Reform, Housing and Urban Development Act and the 1996 Housing Act, have added greatly to the rights of flat owners. Two others, the 1988 Housing Act and the 1989 Local Government and Housing Act introduced changes which, on balance, favoured landlords. Such frequent changes in the law can be difficult to follow and grasp. And as with much new law, it can be hard to explain accurately how it will work in practice and how it might be interpreted by the courts.

A summary of a flat owner's rights

> To purchase the freehold of your building with others.
> To extend your lease.
> To purchase your landlord's interest with others.
> To have your building managed properly.
> To be consulted about major works, etc.
> To receive information about service charges and to monitor your landlord's performance.

Like all human relationships, that between flat owner and landlord can go wrong. Not all landlords are good landlords. Some are difficult to contact, others cannot be found at all, some fail to carry out their repairing and other responsibilities and others overcharge for services. There are frequent disputes about the upkeep and cleaning of blocks of flats and the cost of repairs. Abuses by landlords remain widespread. Most frequent are complaints about repairs and difficulties in contacting the landlord; followed by complaints about service charges.

A report in the mid-1980s highlighted the poor quality of management in many large blocks of flats, including a failure to repair, collect service charges and properly insure the building. This report was instrumental in leading to a change in legislation through the 1987 Landlord and Tenant Act although its impact was later found to be marginal. Older or larger blocks and conversions tended to have greater problems. In the early 1990s a study which concentrated on small blocks and conversions found that problems still existed. The main ones were mismanagement and badly-worded leases. Further research in the 1990s confirmed that the 1987 Act has had a limited impact and was sceptical about the benefits of the 1993 Act, particularly for those living in blocks in poor repair with significant management problems.

Even if a landlord is conscientious and reliable, problems can still arise if, for example, there are technical defects in the lease or the managing agents employed by the landlord do not carry out their duties responsibly. Additional problems are created for flat owners, such as a difficulty in selling their property, when their lease only has a short time left to run.

The purpose of this book is to provide a practical guide for flat owners on how to deal with these and similar problems. It covers:

> The special points to look out for when buying a flat and dealing with mortgage problems.
> The long residential leasehold system including how to vary your lease and what happens when your lease expires.
> Your rights over service charges.
> Your right to buy the freehold of your building collectively at any time.
> Your right to extend your lease.
> Your right to buy your landlord's interest in your building collectively if your landlord wants to sell.
> Your rights to information and to be consulted about, for example, insurance and managing agents.
> Your rights to seek the appointment of a manager for your building and to compulsorily buy your landlord out.
> The role of leaseholder management companies.
> The alternative methods of settling disputes.

Leases contain many technical and legal terms and phrases which are hard or impossible for most lay people, and some professionals, to understand. A glossary explains the meaning of those in most common use. The book ends with a list of:

> The main Acts of Parliament relevant to flat owners.
> Useful publications.
> Useful addresses.
> The addresses of local Leasehold Valuation Tribunals and Rent Assessment Panels.

Most of what is said about flats in this guide applies equally to a maisonette. A maisonette is, usually, similar to a self-contained flat with its own separate entrance, but on two floors rather than one, with no shared stairway. The law relating to flats also applies in most respects to those flat owners who occupy former local authority or housing association property bought under the right to buy or other legislation.

The law considered in the guide is that applying in England and Wales. Scotland has its own very different, and in many respects superior, legal arrangements to cater for flat ownership. Leasehold ownership is almost unknown in Scotland and the great majority of flats are owned on a form of feudal tenure which is comparable to freehold.

The guide is not aimed, except incidentally, at the owners of leasehold houses, whose right, for example, to buy their freehold or extend their lease is different from that of flat owners. However, leasehold house owners have similar rights to flat owners over, for example, service charges.

The guide is not a legal textbook and it is not intended to be a substitute for professional advice, assistance or representation. It is aimed at intelligent readers who wish to know more about their rights as leaseholders, the sort of problems or difficulties they might face and what they can do about them. Whilst every effort has been made to make the guide as accurate and as up-to-date as possible, the author and publisher are unable to accept responsibility for any errors it may contain. They welcome positive comments, criticism and suggestions which will be taken account of in future editions.

Finally, it should be borne in mind that in the last resort enforcing one's legal rights may mean going to court. Legal action is usually expensive and often protracted. It is preferable to try to avoid it. It is often sensible to try to settle a disagreement informally or to use an alternative method of dispute resolution before contemplating legal action. Reference to a court in the guide is to a County Court in England and Wales unless otherwise stated.

FUTURE CHANGES

Despite all the legislative reforms which were made during the late 1980s and into the 1990s, many experts believe that the leasehold system remains inherently unjust and unsatisfactory. Although much of the protection looks good on paper, some of the reforms have not, for a number of reasons, worked as well as was expected. Despite all the safeguards, bad landlords have found ways to continue with old abuses and have invented some new ones. Leaseholders have found some of the remedies cumbersome, difficult and expensive to use. There are frequent difficulties with managing agents, who are unregulated, as well as with landlords, and there is no form of quality assurance to enable landlords or leaseholder management companies to employ agents with confidence. More generally, there are many inconsistencies, anomalies and gaps in the law, as a result of 30 years of piecemeal and often rushed legislation.

Recognising these concerns, in 1998 the Government published a consultation paper on further leasehold reform, addressing the issue of management, and called for the introduction of a new structure of ownership to be known as 'Commonhold'. A second consultation paper, accompanied by a draft Commonhold and Leasehold Reform Bill, published in August 2000, elaborated on the earlier proposals. At the time of going to press, it had been announced the Bill would form part of the Queen's Speech on 6th December 2000. The prospects for introducing the measures are good.

In summary these reforms would:

> Introduce Commonhold, a new form of tenure for newly-developed blocks of flats, under which occupiers would own their flats individually and, through an association, own and manage the common parts collectively. Commonhold would give flat owners an absolute right of ownership, while having shared ownership of, and shared duties towards, the common parts (for example, the roof, entrance halls, stairs, etc) of the building. It would be possible for existing leasehold blocks to convert to Commonhold, provided all interested parties agreed.

> Simplify the collective enfranchisement and lease extension provisions, including the valuation process.

> Give leaseholders a new 'Right to Manage' as an alternative to collective enfranchisement.

> Improve leaseholders' rights in relation to service charges, variation of leases, forfeiture proceedings and in a number of other areas.

The Commonhold proposals will, the Government hopes, provide a complete answer to many of the problems which have plagued flat owners over the decades. The other reforms would give leaseholders brand-new rights and enhance their existing ones, for the benefit of those who will not be able, or may not wish, to convert to Commonhold.

When might these proposals see the light of day?

Once the Bill has been published, there will be a need for fine-tuning, in the light of the consultation exercise. The Bill will then have to await an opportunity to be introduced in Parliament. A general election may well intervene before the Bill has passed through all the necessary Parliamentary stages. The best answer is: not for many months.

1   Long residential leases

Introduction

If you own your home you may either own the freehold or the lease of the property. A freeholder is the absolute owner. Unless the property is mortgaged, sold or rented to someone else, no one can get greater rights over the property than the freeholder. House owners are typically freeholders although there remain a large number of leasehold houses. Leases are legally-binding contracts agreed between two parties – usually the freeholder and the original leaseholder. A leaseholder is the owner of the property for a fixed period of time only. Almost all flat and maisonette owners are leaseholders of their homes. Somebody else owns the freehold of the property; this may be an individual, a private company or even all the leaseholders collectively.

This chapter explains:

> some of the specific points to consider when buying a flat
> the leasehold system
> how to change a lease
> what happens when leases expire
> what 'forfeiture' means.

There is a short final section providing practical advice if you experience financial difficulties and have trouble paying your mortgage.

Maisonettes

Two common types of 'maisonette' are found in Britain. One type is a self-contained dwelling forming part of a building with accommodation on two floors. In effect, this is a two-floor flat. In the United States, they are known as 'duplexes'. This type of maisonette is a flat in law.

The second is a type of building which is familiar in southern England. Externally, it looks like a single house, but the ground and first floors are built to be separately occupied. They do not inter-connect, and each has their own front door at ground level. Each floor is called a 'maisonette'. Such properties have been treated as 'a house' for individual leasehold enfranchisement. Nevertheless, many of the rights covered in this book, except possibly those relating to collective enfranchisement and the right of first refusal, apply equally to this kind of maisonette. Owners of this type of property who are contemplating action of any kind should first seek expert legal advice about their rights in law.

Buying a flat

The purchase process is similar to that when a house is bought and sold, but the relationship between the freeholder and flat owner brings with it a variety of different considerations and added legal complications. What the new owner actually buys from the vendor is the lease to the flat rather than the flat itself. The freehold of the building in which the flat is situated is owned by somebody else. And freeholds can be bought and sold just as flats can be bought and sold. In fact, some people trade in residential freeholds, usually those of large blocks, as a form of investment.

The freeholder originally sold the right to occupy the flat in return for a substantial sum but retains many rights and obligations over the premises. The flat owner buys the temporary ownership of the flat subject to a large and varied number of obligations, restrictions and liabilities. If you are a first-time buyer, you should try to understand what the main ones are.

Typical obligations of flat owners include:

> to pay an annual ground rent – usually this is a small sum, sometimes it is nothing
> to pay an annual service or maintenance charge to cover, for example, the cost of insurance, cleaning and maintenance of the common parts
> to pay for major repairs to the fabric of the property
> to look after the property
> to observe the terms of the lease regarding alterations to their flat, nuisance behaviour, etc

Some blocks of flats are collectively owned and/or managed by the flat owners themselves; most are owned and managed by someone who does not live in the property. You should find out who owns and runs the property as a whole and, if the block is collectively managed, decide whether you are prepared to contribute to the management yourself. Although attendance at meetings, etc, is always voluntary, so is buying a flat in a self-managed block! Resident-managed blocks should be looked after better and more economically whilst residents only discuss and decide the kinds of issues – say, when to get the exterior painted – an individual house owner would do for themselves anyway. More and more flat owners are deciding to run their blocks for themselves. Often, this is because the original freeholder or landlord did not look after the building properly or tried to impose excessive service charges.

If you are buying a new flat or a flat which has not been leased before you are entitled, in theory at least, to negotiate any terms that you wish. In practice, however, this can be difficult. There are certain terms which are almost always included in residential leases (see *Normal clauses included in long leases,* page 27). Furthermore, the vendor may only be prepared to sell the flat to you if you agree to certain terms. As there is generally a shortage of accommodation, freeholders selling flats are generally in a stronger position than people wanting to buy, so the terms of leases tend to favour them. Even so, it is important to try to ensure that the lease gives you the rights you need to live in the flat securely and comfortably. If you do not understand or are concerned about something, ask your solicitor or conveyancer for advice. Leases, like all legal documents, can contain errors. It can be very difficult for a flat owner to sell their flat if the lease is seriously defective.

If you are buying a flat from an existing flat owner, the lease is transferred to you with all its existing rights and obligations. The transfer or sale of a lease is called an 'assignment'. It is far more difficult to renegotiate the terms of an existing lease with a freeholder, but occasionally this is possible by entering into a further document called a 'Deed of Variation'. If you cannot agree, you may be able to go to court to get an order changing the terms of the lease (see *Varying leases,* page 28).

The different terms used when dealing with flats

Ordinary language	Legal language
Flat owner, owner-occupier, home owner	Tenant, long leaseholder, lessee
Building/block owner	Landlord, lessor, freeholder

Another question on which you should satisfy yourself before purchase is the length of the term remaining on the lease. Leases on flats are for a fixed number of years; typically originally 99 or 125 years when granted. You need to know how many years are left to run on the lease. Although a flat with a short outstanding term may be relatively cheap to buy, it may be difficult to obtain a mortgage on it. People are used to the idea of property constantly appreciating in value. However, at a certain stage – say less than 30 years left to run – that is not necessarily true of a leasehold flat. And if the remaining term is very short, it may prove impossible to sell at all. The lease will expire automatically at the end of the term although most leaseholders have a right to stay on as renting tenants at the end of the lease (see *What happens when leases expire?* page 31). Many leaseholders have the right to extend their lease (see Chapter 5).

You should, like any other potential home buyer, have a survey of the property carried out by a qualified surveyor. In older blocks, it is advisable to have a full structural survey done, or as full a survey as possible, and not one of the cheaper alternatives promoted by many mortgage lenders.

You should try to speak to other residents or, if there is one, the secretary of the tenants' or leaseholders' association. Find out what relationship they have with the landlord, if there is one, and with the managing agent. Ask if there are any disputes outstanding or major works planned. You can also try to ring the landlord or managing agent and ask any questions you have about the property. Get the managing agent to explain how the property is managed. Find out how much the service charge is, if this information has not already been provided, and what it covers. If the block is collectively managed by the residents themselves, contact the Company Secretary and ask about the administrative arrangements, major works, etc.

The leasehold system

Leases set out a flat owner's rights and responsibilities. Few flat owners ever read their leases; fewer still understand them. Like most home buyers faced with complicated-looking documents, such as title deeds or mortgage agreements, this is often left to the solicitor or conveyancer. In the case of leases this can be a mistake because, if the truth be told, many professionals do not check them thoroughly enough either or simply take them for granted. Most residential property bought and sold is freehold not leasehold. There is little need for anyone – professional or layperson – to understand either the concept, the principles or the detail of a lease.

Residential leases are undoubtedly heavy going. English law has developed a jargon of legal terms and expressions which are incomprehensible to most people. This is especially true of leases and of the various clauses or covenants which are part of them. Coming to grips with some of this language is a necessary evil and certain important concepts and principles do need to be grasped. All flat owners should, at the very least, understand what these are. These are:

> The person who creates or grants a lease (the words are interchangeable) is known as the lessor or landlord; the person to whom it is granted is the lessee, leaseholder or tenant. A landlord may be the freeholder of the building or may themselves be a leaseholder. In this book the term **flat owner** is used to describe a lessee, a leaseholder or a tenant with a long lease who owns or is buying a flat or maisonette, although this is not a legal term. Flat owners may hold their lease direct from the freeholder or from an intermediate leaseholder. When this guide refers to 'your landlord' this means, unless otherwise stated, your immediate landlord.

> When a lease is created, the landlord retains the freehold of the property, unless the landlord is also a leaseholder themselves. This is known as the landlord's 'reversion' because at the end of the lease, the property reverts back to the landlord, subject to certain exceptions. At its simplest, therefore, at any one time there are two owners of the property – the landlord and the flat owner – but each owns a different interest. One owns the freehold, the other the leasehold.

If there are intermediate leases, then there can be many more people with an interest in the property. Although there can only be one freehold owner of a building, there can be any number of leases on all or separate parts of it.

Example

Company A owns the freehold of a building with lots of flats. In 1994 it granted a lease of the whole block to Company B for 125 years. In 1995 Company B started to sell individual flats in the building on 99 year leases. In this situation Company A is the 'head' lessor. Company B is the 'head' lessee. Individual flat owners are 'sub or under-lessees'. Company B is the direct or immediate landlord and Company A is the superior landlord of the flat owners. In order to exercise their rights, it is important that flat owners can identify the ownership of the leases and the freehold of their block.

> A landlord can sell the freehold, sell the lease or grant a new lease on their property and the flat owner can sell or assign the remaining period of their lease. Flat owners are usually prevented from granting a further long lease on their flat. The effect of such assignments is that a new landlord or a new flat owner steps into the shoes of the original parties. This can happen any number of times during the course of a lease.

> The rights and duties of flat owners are governed by the leases which they have bought subject to the rights which the freeholder retains in the lease. Leases may compel flat owners to do positive things such as to pay a service charge and allow landlords to do things such as entering the flat to carry out an inspection or compel them to do other things such as insuring the building containing the flat. Flat owners can do more or less whatever they want in their flat provided they do not break the terms of their lease.

WHAT ARE LEASES?

Unlike a freehold which gives the buyer what is, in effect, complete ownership of the land and the building(s) on it for ever, a lease confers only a limited ownership of the property for a fixed period of time. Your lease will allow you to occupy your flat for a fixed number of years – known as the 'term'. The lease diminishes from the term which was originally granted and the outstanding term will depend on what was left when you took over the lease.

Example

A person buys a flat in 1999. The term of the lease was 125 years when originally granted in 1955. The outstanding term is 81 years.

A lease is carved out of the freehold of the landlord and can take a number of forms. At one end of the spectrum there is, for example, the tenancy of a furnished bed-sit, providing short-term accommodation at a weekly rent; at the other is the long-term lease bought for a large capital sum or premium, with only a nominal ground rent payable.

This book is primarily aimed at flat owners with a long lease or tenancy on their home – however long there remains to run on it – and not at tenants who have short leases or tenancies except incidentally. In law, most maisonettes are flats so this book also applies to people who own or are buying a maisonette.

For a tenancy to arise, several conditions must be met:

> there must be a landlord and a tenant;
> there must be 'exclusive possession' which is, essentially, the right to occupy the premises to the exclusion of all others, including the landlord;
> there must be identifiable land;
> the grant must be for a definite period;
> the landlord must retain a 'reversion', the right to get possession when the tenancy expires, but this may subsequently be sold.

To qualify as a 'long' tenancy three further conditions must be satisfied:

1. A long tenancy is a tenancy originally granted for a term exceeding 21 years, whether or not it has been subsequently extended. Typical terms for a long tenancy are 99, 125 or 999 years.
2. It must be at a low rent. If the tenancy was entered into before 1 April 1990, the rent payable must be less than two-thirds of the rateable value of the property. If the tenancy was entered into on or after that date, the rent payable must be:
   > £1,000 or less a year if the property is in Greater London, or
   > £250 or less a year if the property is elsewhere.
3. It must satisfy the 'qualifying condition'. In simple terms, this means that it is excluded from Rent Act or Housing Act protection. This is not, in fact, a separate condition. It is, rather, a consequence of the second condition.

In most situations there is no doubt that a flat owner has a valid long lease. Almost all flats in England and Wales are owned leasehold. The lease is an important document and you should make sure that you obtain and keep a copy. It sets out the rights and duties of the landlord and the leaseholder. It will normally define who is responsible for looking after the different parts of the building, for insurance, and may restrict how the property may be used (for example, business activities may be banned). The lease will usually require flat owners to reimburse the landlord for any expenditure they make on the building, through a regular service charge (see *Normal clauses included in long leases,* page 27).

Ground rents

The low or 'ground rent' payable under a long residential lease is often a modest sum; perhaps £50 or £100 a year. The precise amount or some method of calculating it will be stated in the lease. Since ground rents are normally insignificant, the question arises as to why they are there at all. There are two reasons. An annual payment constitutes a 'consideration' in law without which there can be no valid contract, and a lease is, after all, a rather detailed contract. Second, because such a relatively small sum is unlikely to affect the sale price, many landlords take the view that as long as it is not actually more bother than it is worth, they may as well collect it. Although a ground rent is usually a nominal amount, it is important that it is paid promptly. Many leases entitle the landlord to commence court proceedings to bring the lease to an end if the rent is in arrears even for only a short period (see *Forfeiture,* page 33).

There are examples of ground rents which were clearly introduced purely to comply with the first criterion. A 'peppercorn rent' (i.e. nothing) is one. More recently, some landlords have introduced ground rents set at an initial figure which is not altogether nominal and which rises at intervals. They may rise to a predetermined amount or they may be subject to a review based on a percentage of capital or rental value. Ground rents on long leases are limited by the low rent condition discussed earlier. If a ground rent is above the relevant amount, the tenancy will not be 'a long tenancy at a low rent'. It may in fact be a regulated tenancy falling within the Rent Act or an assured tenancy falling within the Housing Act.

Landlords and flat owners are bound by all the terms of a lease unless both agree to change any of them. In some circumstances certain terms of a lease may be changed in the absence of agreement (see *Varying leases,* page 28). If the lease states that either the landlord or the flat owner must do something, then they must do so.

If one party breaks a term of the lease, then the other party can take action. For example, if the lease states that the landlord must repair a specific part of the property and this is not done, then the flat owner can get a court to order the landlord to do the repairs and, perhaps, pay compensation (see Chapter 6). On the other hand, one party may go to court to get an order that the other party stop doing something (for example, running a business from their flat) which is prohibited by the lease. Generally landlords and flat owners are not obliged to do particular things unless there is a specific covenant or clause in the lease stating that they must do so. There are, however, some exceptions:

1. Some of the clauses in the lease may be overridden by an Act of Parliament. For example, the obligation of a flat owner to pay a particular amount of service charge may be overridden by the provisions of the 1985 Landlord and Tenant Act (see Chapter 2). Similarly, the common law right of a landlord to evict a flat owner for breaking a clause of the lease (the legal phrase is 'to re-enter' and 'forfeit' the lease) is limited by the provisions of the 1977 Protection from Eviction Act as amended and by other statutory protection for leaseholders (see *Forfeiture*, page 33).

Leasehold flats and the public sector

Some of the rights flat owners have do not apply to the owners of properties held on leases from public sector bodies and some charities. In particular, if your landlord is a local authority or a registered social landlord (which includes most housing associations and housing action trusts) you do not have a right of first refusal (see Chapter 4). There are other important exemptions for public bodies and charities. Where relevant, these are mentioned in the text.

2. There may be some rights read into a lease even though they are not specifically spelt out in it. A right or an obligation which is read into a lease or other document in this way is known as an 'implied' right or obligation. Some of these implied rights are called 'easements'. An easement is a right which a property owner is entitled to exercise over other property (for example, a right of way). Generally, rights are only

read into leases if a court considers that they are both absolutely necessary to make the contract work and, in all the circumstances, reasonable. For example, if a flat owner would not be able to live normally in the flat if these rights were not included, or if a court considers that the rights are so obvious that everyone would have included them in the lease if they had thought about them at the time the lease was granted. Some well-established implied rights or obligations include:

> The right to support – a landlord cannot demolish or neglect the lower floors if this would mean that an owner's flat on an upper floor would collapse.

> Access through the hall, lift, stairs, drives and entrance – a landlord cannot do anything which stops or makes it substantially more difficult for the flat owner to get into their flat.

> The right to the continuation of existing services – a landlord cannot do anything which leads to the disconnection or termination of existing services such as gas, water, electricity, telephone, postal delivery, etc. This does not apply to personal services such as caretaking. If a caretaker is to be provided, there should be a specific clause to that effect in the lease.

> Repair and upkeep of common parts – in some cases there may be an implied obligation that a landlord maintains stairs, lifts, lighting in halls, rubbish chutes, etc.
A landlord also has an implied duty to ensure that people using the common parts are reasonably safe from injury arising from defects to the building. In general, a landlord will be able to pass on the costs of this obligation in service charges (see Chapter 2).

There is no right to privacy read into a lease. However, a landlord only has a right to come into a flat in accordance with specific terms set out in a lease.

NORMAL CLAUSES INCLUDED IN LONG LEASES

There is not enough space to give a full guide to all the terms and conditions usually found in a lease. The following list contains some of the more important clauses which are normally included:

> Description of the property – the flat may be described simply in words, or in words together with a plan. It is obviously important that this is done precisely so that it is clear what the resident owns. Most leases state who is responsible for the walls, ceilings and floors of a flat.

> The price paid by the original flat owner, the ground rent payable and how the service charge is calculated.

> The length of the lease when it was originally granted and the date when it was granted.

> The services which the landlord is obliged to provide (for example, central heating, hot water, cleaning and lighting of the common parts).

> Details about other parts of the building which the flat owner is allowed to use (for example, halls, car parking spaces, garden).

> Details of who is allowed access to the flat (for example, neighbouring flat owners if this is necessary to carry out repairs to their flat, landlord's surveyor).

> Repairing and redecorating obligations – often leases make flat owners responsible for repairs and decorations to their flat and sometimes for the external walls of the flat. The landlord should always be responsible for repairs to those parts of the building which are not leased.

> A clause allowing the landlord to 're-enter' the flat if the flat owner breaks any of the obligations contained in the lease (see *Forfeiture*, page 33).

> Clauses relating to the use of the flat (for example, forbidding business activities, not to make structural alterations without permission, provisions about sub-letting).

> A clause forbidding leaseholders to cause a nuisance, annoyance or disturbance.

> Insurance – there should be an obligation on someone to keep the whole building insured. This is usually the landlord.
> A clause that other owners or occupiers in the building will have to observe similar clauses in their leases and that other leases in the building will contain similar clauses.

Handy hints

> Make sure you understand as clearly as possible the main terms of your lease – which states your rights and responsibilities – before you buy your flat.
> Keep a copy of your lease.
> When you get a copy of the lease, read through each clause and write a short summary of each, in plain English, in the margin of a spare copy of the lease.
> Ask your solicitor or someone with expert knowledge to explain anything in the lease you do not understand.

Varying leases

Leases can be varied at any time with the mutual agreement of all the parties concerned. However, if agreement cannot be reached, the 1987 Landlord and Tenant Act gives flat owners and landlords the right to ask a court to make an order varying the lease. A lease can be varied by a court if it is defective in certain ways relating to the management of the block or the service charges or if a majority of the parties want a change but a small minority have not given their consent.

It would only be sensible to commence legal action if the change you want is an important one. The court will expect you to have first tried to get the lease changed by agreement with your landlord. Your first step should be to write to the landlord to find out if they will agree to the change(s) you want. Always keep copies of any letters in case you need to show them to the court subsequently. If you do have the right to go to court, your landlord may be willing to agree to the lease being changed to avoid the risk and expense of a court case. It is particularly important to get expert legal advice before deciding to go to court to get a lease varied.

WHO CAN GO TO COURT?

The length of the lease when originally granted must exceed 21 years unless it was granted by a local authority or another public sector landlord as a result of a flat owner exercising their statutory right to buy; in which case the lease need not be of any particular length. If a leaseholder has three or more flats in a block, they are not able to require a court to vary their lease.

Example

'Unfortunately, in our lease it does say we should have Reserves, but it says "after consultation..." Now what on earth does that mean? Because all (the managing agents do) is produce these large documents to us and they say, "We'd like to talk to you about this, and this is what we're going to do..."; *fait accompli,* and it's done, we can't argue about it.'

– Resident, large converted block in Berkshire

WHAT TYPE OF DEFECTS?

The following are the most important defective items in a lease which can be corrected by a court:

> The repair or maintenance of the flat, the block, or any land or building which is leased to the flat owner and any installations or services. For example, a court could change the lease to require a landlord to keep the structure of the block, including the roof, walls and foundations, in repair if the lease did not require this. Or the lease could be varied to ensure that a landlord has to maintain a block's hot water and heating system. Or a court could impose obligations on a landlord to clean and light the common parts.

> The insurance of the property. A court may vary the lease to compel a landlord to insure the building or place a landlord under an obligation to take out sufficient insurance cover to allow the

whole block to be rebuilt if it was destroyed or seriously damaged (see *Insurance,* page 113).

> The calculation of service charges. A court can vary a lease to ensure that a landlord cannot recover from the flat owners in service charges more than has been spent on the building including management charges. A court might also be able to alter the lease to ensure that service charges are fairly calculated and apportioned between the flat owners (see Chapter 2).

> The recovery of expenditure under the lease. For example, to allow a landlord to be recompensed for the costs incurred in meeting one of their obligations under the lease.

The law allows the flat owner to ask a court not only to change their own lease but also the leases of other flat owners if a majority agree and if it would be sensible for them all to be changed in a similar way, for example, if a court is being asked to require the landlord to light the common parts of a block of flats and the other flat owners also own flats in the same block.

Applications by a large majority of leaseholders

Two or more long leases of flats can be varied by a court if a large majority of the flat owners agree to the change and only a small minority object.

If the application relates to eight or fewer leases, all, or all but one, of the parties, including the landlord, must agree to the application. If the application relates to more than eight leases, at least 75 per cent of the parties concerned must consent to it, and it must not be opposed by more than 10 per cent of them.

The application must refer to long leases of flats held from the same landlord, but the flats do not have to be in the same building and neither do the leases have to be drafted in identical terms.

Even if a lease is defective in one of the ways mentioned, a court may refuse to change it. It may also only be willing to change the lease in the way requested by a flat owner if compensation for the change is paid to the landlord (for example, if the change would cause the landlord financial loss). A court may also insist on the lease being changed to allow the landlord to recover the cost of any new obligations from the flat owner as a service charge.

What happens when leases expire?

All leases come to an end sometime. All leases, when drafted, set out the length of the term of years agreed and its starting date. The exact date of expiry, if not explicitly stated, can easily be determined. A flat owner with a long fixed-term lease is often described as an 'owner-occupier' and is regarded as having more in common with a freehold house owner than with a tenant. A flat owner's main worry is more likely to be whether they can meet the mortgage and the other costs associated with property ownership than whether the landlord is likely to repossess their flat. If there are 90 years left to run on a lease, what happens when that term ends may appear a remote prospect. When there are only five years left, though, it will be a real cause for concern. If the flat owner wishes to sell, they may find it impossible to get a decent price. Or the flat owner is not sure if they will be able to remain in the property when their lease expires.

In many cases, a lease will not expire on the last day of the term originally granted. A flat owner may negotiate a new lease with the landlord before the expiry date. Or the flat owner may exercise their statutory right to have their lease extended (see Chapter 5) or to purchase the freehold of their block collectively, which is often followed by the new owners granting themselves lease extensions (see Chapter 3). The extension of long leaseholders' rights by the 1993 Leasehold Reform, Housing and Urban Development Act has made it much less likely that long leases will ever expire.

Nevertheless some will. Prior to the mid-1950s there was no statutory protection for long leaseholders on the termination of their lease: the situation was governed by the common law. The 1954 Landlord and Tenant Act introduced provisions giving long leaseholders similar protection to that already available to periodic and short fixed-term tenants under the Rent Acts. The

Rent Acts were superseded much later by the 1988 Housing Act which introduced the assured tenancy regime into the private sector. Correspondingly, new provisions were introduced to govern long leases granted after the enactment of the 1988 Housing Act. These provisions are contained in the 1989 Local Government and Housing Act. This would have meant that there were two codes affecting long leases running in parallel for many years into the next century. The 1989 Act foresaw this and provided a cut-off point. From 15 January 1999, virtually all long leases are governed by the 1989 Act regardless of when they were granted.

Although a landlord may wish a flat owner to vacate the premises when the lease expires, the flat owner will be able to remain in lawful occupation. The flat owner will no longer own their home – their lease has expired – but will have become an assured tenant paying a market rent to their landlord. A landlord is only able to get a possession order from a court, necessary for lawful eviction, on one or more of the grounds specified in the Act. This is, of course, not as good as a another fixed-term long lease but it is better than being made homeless.

An astute flat owner, towards the end of a long lease, may seek to negotiate a large capital sum as an incentive to leave the flat which may be the only way their landlord can get vacant possession of the property, or they may be able to negotiate a new lease from the advantageous position of being in possession.

A landlord must serve a notice on the flat owner stating whether they propose to create a monthly assured tenancy or intend to seek possession of the flat. The flat owner has two months to respond to a landlord's notice proposing an assured tenancy. The landlord may apply for possession when the long lease ends or at any time afterwards. Briefly, the main grounds for possession which are likely to apply when a long lease ends are:

Mandatory
> The landlord intends to demolish or reconstruct the whole or a substantial part of the building.

Discretionary
> Suitable alternative accommodation is offered to the former flat owner.
> Some rent arrears.

> Persistent delay in payment of rent.
> Breach of obligation of the tenancy.
> Deterioration of condition of the property.
> Causing nuisance or annoyance to adjoining occupiers; or being convicted of using the property for immoral or illegal purposes.
> Domestic violence.
> The accommodation is wanted for the landlord or a close relative of the landlord.

Under the discretionary grounds, a court will only evict a former flat owner if it is reasonable to do so. If the landlord fails to establish any of the grounds for possession, the former flat owner is entitled to remain in possession and go on living there. Many leases affected by this legislation will not be coming to an end for a long time. The vast majority of flat owners will have been able to exercise their rights to the collective purchase of the freehold (see Chapter 3) or to extend their lease (see Chapter 4).

Forfeiture

If a flat owner breaks any of the terms of their lease, the landlord may have a right to forfeit the lease and recover possession of the property. Most well-drafted leases contain a clause saying that the landlord is entitled to 're-enter' the property and 'forfeit' (put an end to) the lease in certain situations. Forfeiture is not available unless there is such a clause. Forfeiture is the legal term used when a landlord brings a lease to an end before it would normally expire. It is of special importance in long leases which, unlike other kinds of tenancy, cannot be ended by a notice to quit. Many leases state that the lease can be forfeited if the ground rent or service charge is in arrears or if the flat owner has broken some other term of the lease. This is, of course, why it is very important for flat owners to understand what the clauses in their lease mean.

Although many leases state that a landlord is entitled to 're-enter forthwith' (this means immediately), the 1977 Protection from Eviction Act requires a landlord who wishes to end a lease to first go to a court for a possession order. It is a criminal offence, punishable by fine or imprisonment, for a landlord to evict or attempt to evict a flat owner without first going to court. A flat owner who has been illegally evicted can get a court to reinstate them in their home and can also claim damages from their landlord. In some circumstances these can be substantial.

Before you start to panic because you have just forgotten to make your last service charge payment, it should be emphasised that forfeiture is not primarily a means of ending a lease and evicting a flat owner but a legal method to allow a landlord to enforce their rights. The procedure involved with forfeiture is awkward and complicated. Even if a landlord does go to court to forfeit the lease, because of its potentially far reaching effects several Acts of Parliament offer protection to flat owners:

> If your landlord claims possession for arrears of ground rent, a formal demand for the money owing must have been made, unless the lease specifically states that it can be forfeited whether or not the ground rent has been formally demanded.

> If you have a dispute with your landlord about service charges, forfeiture proceedings cannot be started for non-payment of service charges until it has been found that the service charge is lawfully due, by agreement or admission of the flat owner or by decision of the court or Tribunal (see Chapter 2).

> If your landlord claims possession on other grounds (for example, breaking a clause in the lease which states that the property should only be used for residential and not for business purposes), your landlord must first serve a formal notice telling you about your breach of the clause and giving you an opportunity to put things right.

> If possession proceedings are brought for arrears of ground rent or service charges, the proceedings are automatically stopped if all money owing (including the landlord's legal costs) is paid into the court at least five days before the hearing. Even after a court hearing to forfeit a lease, a flat owner still has four weeks to pay all the money due. If the money is paid within the time limit, the lease continues as before. If the money is not paid

within that time, the lease is brought to an end and a flat owner can be evicted.

> If a landlord goes to court for the breach of any other clause in the lease, a court has wide discretion to stop the lease from being brought to an end. This is usually done if the flat owner has stopped breaking the terms of the lease and promises not to do so again in the future.

Forfeiture is rare if the breach of contract can be remedied. But landlords sometimes try to exploit the threat of forfeiture. If your landlord is threatening you with forfeiture proceedings, it is vital that you seek expert advice from a solicitor or other expert quickly. There may be a defence which you are not aware of. But if you fight a case and the court says there is no defence, you may have to pay your landlord's legal costs as well as your own and lose your home too.

Example

A flat owner agreed to pay by instalments to cover the cost of work to his block's footpaths. Because he felt the work was not satisfactory, although the landlord disagreed, he stopped making his payments. The landlord responded by asking for the full amount owing and threatened forfeiture if it was not paid. The flat owner offered to recommence his instalments but the landlord refused and again threatened forfeiture.

Difficulty paying your mortgage

If you, for example, fall ill, lose your job or experience a reduced income and have difficulty paying your mortgage, you may be in danger of losing your home. You should always contact your mortgage lender to discuss your options without delay. Your chief options are to:

> cut your mortgage costs, and/or
> increase your income.

Mortgage lenders may be prepared to:

> Reduce or defer payments for a limited period.
> Lengthen your term or change the type of mortgage to reduce your monthly payments.
> Allow you to take in a lodger or sub-let your flat.

> Arrange for you to move to a cheaper property despite being in arrears.

Mortgage lenders have agreed a code of practice and are expected to consider cases of financial difficulty and mortgage arrears sympathetically. A few run 'mortgage rescue' schemes under which an owner can remain in their flat as a tenant, rather than lose their home altogether. Up to £62.50 of weekly income from renting out a room to a lodger is not liable for taxation. You may also be able to reduce your payments by re-mortgaging your flat with a different lender.

There is a wide range of social security benefits available to top up your income, some of which you may be entitled to claim. You should not forget to check your mortgage protection insurance policy, if you have one, for details of the help it can offer.

You should seek advice from your local Benefits Agency office, Jobcentre, Citizens Advice Bureau or similar if you are unable to work at all or are unable to work full-time. You may be entitled to social security help with your housing and other costs.

BENEFITS FOR HOME OWNERS

Some home owners can get help with their housing costs as well as cash for their own and their family's needs from either the income support or the income-based jobseeker's allowance schemes. Both are social security benefits to help people whose income is below a certain level and who generally are not working 16 hours or more a week. Home owners who qualify only for contribution-based jobseeker's allowance – which used to be known as unemployment benefit – cannot get any help with their housing costs.

Income support/income-based jobseeker's allowance can be paid to top up other benefits, including contribution-based jobseeker's allowance, earnings from part-time work and to someone who has no money coming in at all. And so housing costs can sometimes be met to help homeowners who qualify for contribution-based jobseeker's allowance.

Income support is claimed at the Department of Social Security's local Benefits Agency/social security office. Jobseeker's allowance is claimed at the local Jobcentre. Social security help with mortgage interest is normally paid direct to the lender.

If you think that you might qualify for help you should claim without delay. Interest on mortgage arrears is not eligible for help.

Reminder

Only home owners who get either income support or income-based jobseeker's allowance can qualify for help with their housing costs. In some cases income-based jobseeker's allowance can be paid to top up contribution-based jobseeker's allowance. In such cases, home owners can get help with their housing costs.

HOW DO YOU GET EITHER INCOME SUPPORT OR INCOME-BASED JOBSEEKER'S ALLOWANCE?

There are different rules for each benefit. To get income support you must:

> not be working 16 hours or more a week*
> be at least 16 years old
> normally not be in full-time education
> have income and savings below a certain level

and not be required to be available for work because, for example, you are

> sick or disabled
> a lone parent or foster parent
> 60 or over
> getting invalid care allowance for looking after someone.

To get income-based jobseeker's allowance you must:

> be capable of, actively seeking and available for work
> be out of work or working less than 16 hours a week*
> agree and sign a jobseeker's agreement
> normally be at least 18 years old
> not be in full-time education
> have income and savings below a certain level

if claiming for a partner they must be out of work or working less than 24 hours a week

Working more than 16 hours a week?

Home owners who work 16 hours a week or more, have children and are on a low income may qualify for help under the Working Families Tax Credit scheme. There is a similar scheme called Disabled Person's Tax Credit for low-paid workers who have a disability but, in this case, you do not need to have children. Both benefits top up your income from work. In both cases, you must not have savings above a fixed amount.

The amount of help you get depends on your income, how many children you have and their ages. You can get a claim pack from your local Benefits Agency or a Post Office.

On top of these rules, there are a number of exclusions, restrictions and limitations from all or part of income support and income-based jobseeker's allowance for housing costs. You cannot get any help with capital repayments or the cost of associated insurance premiums, including the insurance element of an endowment mortgage. But you can get help with your ground rent and service charges. If you have taken out a loan to buy the freehold of your block, you can get help to cover this too.

Chief restrictions

For most people there is a waiting period before housing costs can be paid.

> **Aged over 60** – no waiting period.
> **Payments under a co-ownership scheme** – no waiting period.
> **Existing borrowers** – 8 weeks.
> **New borrowers** – 39 weeks.

EXISTING BORROWERS

If your housing costs began before 2 October 1995 or if you have re-mortgaged your existing property with the same lender without borrowing additional money after 1 October 1995 you get:

> No help with housing costs for the first 8 weeks of your claim.
> 50 per cent of housing costs for the next 18 weeks.
> 100 per cent of housing costs after 26 weeks.

NEW BORROWERS

If your housing costs began after 1 October 1995 you get:

> No help with housing costs for the first 39 weeks of your claim.
> 100 per cent of housing costs after 39 weeks.

EXCEPTIONS

If you are a new borrower but are in one of the following groups you are treated the same as an existing borrower:

> Carers.
> Prisoners on remand.
> People whose mortgage protection policy will not pay because the claim has been made because of a pre-existing medical condition or because of a condition related to HIV or AIDS.
> People who claim as a consequence of the death of their partner or because they have been abandoned by their partner, and who have one or more children aged under 16.

Chief limitations

> Payments of mortgage interest are normally calculated using a standard rate of interest, not the rate actually paid.
> There is also a ceiling of £100,000 on the amount of a mortgage which can be helped.
> In some cases, mortgages below the appropriate ceiling can still be considered excessive and benefit reduced.

Other help for home owners

COUNCIL TAX BENEFIT

Council tax benefit is a social security benefit which helps people with their council tax. The scheme is run by your local council. If you are eligible, you will either have to pay less council tax or none at all. People on income support or income-based jobseeker's allowance can get council tax benefit to cover all their council tax. Council tax benefit is also available to anyone on a low income. But you cannot usually get council tax benefit if you have more than £16,000 in savings. If you claim income support or income-based jobseeker's allowance you can claim council tax benefit at the same time. If you are not getting either benefit you can get a council tax benefit claim form from your local council.

SOCIAL FUND LOAN

The social fund helps people with expenses which are difficult to pay for out of regular benefit income. You may be able to get a Budgeting Loan from the Social Fund if you have been on benefit for at least 26 weeks. These interest-free loans are made to help people spread the cost of more expensive items over a longer period. A Budgeting Loan might be made to cover such items as a cooker, bed or other furniture, repairs or removal expenses. The social fund also helps with maternity and funeral expenses, and with the extra costs of heating in cold weather. Apply to your local Benefits Agency/social security office

HOME RENOVATION GRANTS

Your local council can give you a grant to help with the cost of repairing or improving your home. Your home has to be in very poor condition for you to qualify. You must apply before doing any work. People on many benefits can get help with the full cost of the work. There are also special grants for disabled facilities and minor works. Your local council will have more information.

EDUCATION BENEFITS

Some local councils give grants for school uniforms and other items of children's school clothing. The help you receive, if any, may vary considerably and so does the level of income below which you qualify. If you are getting a means-tested benefit, you will also qualify for free school meals. The school secretary or your local council will have more information.

HEALTH BENEFITS

If you are getting a social security benefit or have a low income, you may be able to get help for yourself and for your family with NHS costs, such as prescriptions, dental treatment, sight tests and glasses and with the cost of travelling to hospital. Get more information from your local Benefits Agency/social security office, a hospital, dentist, family doctor or optician.

Getting more information

Further information about social security is available from your local Benefits Agency, Jobcentre, local authority welfare rights office, Citizens Advice Bureau or similar advice agency. The Department of Social Security publishes a series of useful leaflets and booklets which are available free from the above agencies and, usually, also from your local library or Post Office.

2   Service charges

Introduction

Long residential leases usually require flat owners to make two different kinds of regular payment to their landlord:

> > ground rent; and
> > a service charge.

Ground rents are perhaps the most recognisable, although usually insignificant, feature of a long residential lease (see Chapter 1). Service charges are sometimes known as 'maintenance charges', 'service rent' or 'additional rent' but, by law, they cannot be treated as rent properly understood.

Flat owners are responsible for the internal repair, upkeep and decoration of their own flat. Usually their landlord is responsible under the terms of the lease for repairs and maintenance to the block and to any common parts, such as a hall, a lift or garden, and to keep the property insured. In some cases, their landlord may provide other services, such as a caretaker.

In addition to any ground rent, flat owners also have to pay a contribution to their landlord's expenses of providing these services. Service charges cover the costs of this obligation and normally cover the cleaning, decoration, maintenance and repair of the building and common parts, property insurance and any extra services such as caretaking. The service charge is usually the largest item of regular expenditure a flat owner has to meet, other than their mortgage payments. Service charges are often administered and collected by a managing agent who acts on the landlord's behalf. Managing agents will also include their administrative costs in the service charge.

Leases usually require a service charge to be paid annually or often nowadays quarterly or monthly. Unlike a ground rent, a service charge is generally variable from year to year according to the particular services provided. It is common, however, to pay a standard fixed sum, which is corrected either by crediting the flat owner's account or by issuing an additional bill at the end of the year.

Flat owners often complain that their service charge is excessive or that they are not getting value for money. Some also report that it is difficult to find out what their service charge contributions are actually being spent on. There are several stages in finding out how much a landlord may charge for services. First, it is necessary to check the lease itself which should state what items are covered and how the charge is calculated. Second, flat owners are entitled by law to obtain information about their service charge. Third, the law imposes limits on what can be charged and the procedures to be followed. And, fourth, flat owners can challenge a service charge on a number of grounds.

This chapter explains a flat owner's rights in relation to service charges, including:

> service charges and leases
> information about service charges
> the amount of the service charge
> reserve funds
> demands for payment
> challenging service charges.

Service charges and leases

The basic rule is that the cost of an item cannot be recovered from a flat owner unless the lease permits it. If you pay service charges, your lease will set out the items of expenditure for which you are liable. Your lease will also state what share of the overall charge for the block you will be required to pay. Any advance payment must be of a reasonable amount. Your lease may also allow your landlord to operate a 'reserve' or 'sinking fund' towards funding large items of expenditure (see page 54).

You will generally be liable to pay for services even if you do not take advantage of them. For example, you may have to pay for the maintenance of a lift even if you live on the ground floor.

The general rule is that the onus is on a landlord to show that a particular charge is permitted by the lease. If a lease is not explicit on a particular point, it may be that a particular charge could be implied into it but only if it is reasonable. Some leases may have very broad clauses allowing a landlord to provide any services they think fit. Only in such a case could a landlord, for example, introduce and charge for a caretaker against a flat owner's wishes. However, the costs of such a service must be reasonable, and the standard of the service must also be reasonable (see *Amount of service charge,* page 51). Ideally, your solicitor should have drawn your attention to such a wide clause at the time of purchase.

A typical lease will usually require some or all of the service charge to be paid in advance and set a reckoning point – often at the end of the financial or calendar year – when the precise amount is calculated and the excess credited or the deficit invoiced to the flat owner. Sometimes, the lease allows any surplus to remain in a reserve fund. If the lease does not require some of the service charge to be paid in advance, a landlord is only entitled to be paid after the service or work has been provided or done or the money has been spent (see *Amount of service charge,* page 51 for the limitations imposed by the 1985 Landlord and Tenant Act). Money may be payable in advance subject to the trust fund arrangements made mandatory in April 1989 (see *Reserve funds,* page 54).

The inclusion of a profit element, or management charge, in a service charge is often a cause of friction. It is generally perfectly proper, and probably does not need to be expressly mentioned in the list of items for which the lease allows the landlord to charge.

It should be noted that a clause allowing the landlord to set aside funds is just that; a power to put aside some of the service charge income in the year in which it was collected. It is not a power to levy charges in advance for major works. A specific clause on reserve funds is necessary for this which are subject to the trust fund arrangements (see *Reserve funds,* page 54).

Your lease should also specify how the service charge is calculated and apportioned between individual flat owners. The simplest method is to take the total costs incurred in the relevant year and then divide this sum by the number of flats in the building. However, some leases recognise reasons for departing from such a simple formula and, for example, take account of variations in the size of the flats. In some buildings, a few flats may have more restricted access to the common parts than others and so may pay less for services to them. Another common method of calculating a service charge is to make it proportionate to the old rateable value of the individual flats or, increasingly, to a flat's council tax band.

Under the 1987 Landlord and Tenant Act, a court has the power to vary the provisions of a lease relating to the service charge. A lease may be changed if, for example, it does not make satisfactory arrangements for the provision or maintenance of those services reasonably necessary to afford the residents a reasonable standard of accommodation, including safety and security and the condition of the common parts. The Act also has provisions which ensure that all the leases in a block of flats contain the same procedure for the calculation and collection of the service charge. Such variations usually require the majority of those concerned to agree to the application (See *Varying leases,* page 28).

Information about service charges

Flat owners can require their landlord to provide them with information about service charges under statutory rights granted by the 1985 Landlord and Tenant Act, as amended by the 1987 Landlord and Tenant Act and the 1996 Housing Act. You can write to your landlord, either directly or care of the landlord's agent, requesting a written summary of costs incurred in the last service charge accounting year. The secretary of a recognised tenants' association (see *Tenants' associations,* page 117) can make the request on behalf of all the flat owners. If the accounts are not made up on an annual basis, which is unlikely, then you or the secretary can request a written summary for the year ending at the date of the request.

Your landlord must supply the summary either within one month of the request or within six months of the end of the relevant year, whichever is the later. The summary has to show how the costs incurred have been or will be reflected in service charges. It must show which costs, if any, are ones for which the landlord has not had a bill in the relevant year, which costs have been billed but not yet paid and which were billed and paid. It must also show the total amount received from the flat owners as advance payments of service charges which is still standing to their credit at the end of the relevant year.

Since 1997, a recognised tenants' association can appoint a qualified surveyor to advise it on matters relating to service charges. The surveyor has the right to inspect the premises and inspect and copy documents held by the landlord. If your landlord refuses to give your surveyor access to the necessary documents or prevents inspection of the property, the surveyor can apply to a court to force the landlord to comply. In a serious case, you would be well advised to use this right.

If the owners of more than four flats in a block are contributing to the same costs in service charges, then a qualified accountant has to certify that the written summary is fair and supported by accounts, receipts and other documents. The accountant may not be an officer, managing agent, employee or partner of your landlord. A landlord who fails without good reason to provide a summary when requested is guilty of a criminal offence. Local authorities have the power to prosecute in such cases. Summary accounts can be presented in different ways but the example opposite, from a small block of six flats, each paying an equal service charge of £332 in 2000, shows a typical approach.

Example

Dickens Way Management Co Ltd
Service Charge Account
for the year ended 31 March 2000

	2000	1999
Building Insurance	364	367
Electricity Charges	73	90
Communal Cleaning	51	45
Maintenance	40	79
Repairs	756	-
Decoration	-	917
Managing Agent's Fees	465	465
Audit/Accountancy Fees	385	376
Bank charges/Interest	57	45
Sundry Expenses	22	22
Fixed Assets Written Off	1	-
	2,214	2,406
Total Income	1,992	1,992
Withdrawn from Reserves	222	414

Notes to the Account

for the year ended 31 March 2000
Reconciliation of Cash Movements to Total Expenditure

Cash paid during year		1,620
Less: Amounts included in previous accounting period (Accruals brought forward)		(340)
Add: Amounts paid in previous accounting period but not included in previous account (Prepayments brought forward)		70
		1,350
Less: Paid during period but not included in the account (Prepayments carried forward)		(100)
Add Accruals:	Repairs	756	
	Electricity	21	
	Audit/Accountancy Fee	92	
	Managing Agent's Fee	70	
	Maintenance	25	964
Total Expenditure for the year		2,214

Within six months of getting the summary, you or the secretary of the association may write to your landlord, either directly or care of the landlord's agent, requiring them to provide 'reasonable facilities' to inspect and take copies of the accounts, receipts and other documents supporting the summary. Your landlord must make the facilities available for a period of two months, starting not later than one month from the date of the request. You or the secretary are entitled to inspect the documents free of charge and to take copies of them for a reasonable charge. Your landlord is permitted to take the costs of the inspection into account when calculating their management charge. Again, a landlord who fails to allow an inspection is guilty of a criminal offence.

There are similar provisions covering information held by a superior landlord. In particular, if part of the information is needed from a superior landlord then the intermediate landlord is under a duty to go through a similar procedure to obtain it and the superior landlord is under a similar duty to provide it. A failure of the intermediate landlord or the superior landlord to comply with their duties without good reason is a criminal offence.

Management audits

The 1993 Leasehold Reform, Housing and Urban Development Act introduced another way for flat owners to obtain service charge information. Provided enough flat owners – usually not less than two thirds – are prepared to support the application, a landlord can be compelled to agree to a management audit. It is necessary to appoint a qualified accountant or surveyor to carry out such an audit.

The purpose of the audit is to find out if the landlord's management obligations are being performed in an efficient and effective manner, and if the service charges are being spent properly. The auditor has statutory rights to inspect the necessary documents. A court can compel a landlord to comply with a management audit. This right is very powerful but less easy to use than the rights to obtain information.

If it is subsequently decided to challenge some aspect of a landlord's management practices, evidence from an audit will be taken into account and compared with the applicable standard of good management practice set out in the relevant code approved by the Secretary of State (see Chapter 6).

Amount of service charge

The 1985 Landlord and Tenant Act contains limitations on the amount that a flat owner must pay as a service charge. Generally, this statute overrides a lease if there is a conflict. The law defines 'service charges' to mean: 'an amount payable by a tenant (flat owner) of a dwelling as part of or in addition to rent

> which is payable, directly or indirectly, for services, repairs, maintenance, insurance or the landlord's costs of management, and

> the whole of part of which varies or may vary according to the relevant costs.'

Clearly, amounts are only payable if the lease states that they are. 'Relevant costs' includes estimated costs and have to be 'in connection with the matters for which the service charge is payable', including overheads. Costs are still relevant even if they are for a period other than the current service charge year, but see *Demands for payment,* page 56.

The law provides some control over the level of charge. 'Relevant costs' can only be taken into account in working out the service charge to the extent that they are 'reasonably incurred' and only where they are for services or works of a 'reasonable standard'. Payments in advance also have to be reasonable. There has to be a reckoning after the costs have been incurred and any balance either refunded to the flat owner or used to reduce charges in subsequent years. The legislation also declares that a clause in a lease which states that the landlord can decide what is reasonable is void.

Example

Five flat owners have flats in a large house. The landlord's annual bill for service charges includes £600 per flat for cleaning the hall and stairs – a total of £3,000 for the house. The flat owners know the cleaner only visits for an hour once a week. And because the vacuum cleaner has been broken for the past year and the landlord has not had it repaired, the carpets have not actually been cleaned by the cleaner. The flat owners have vacuumed the hall and stairs themselves. In that year, therefore, the charge of £3,000 is not a reasonable relevant cost and the cleaning services are not of a reasonable standard. The flat owners are not legally bound to each pay £600 even though cleaning charges are specified in the lease and the landlord's agents have included the sum in the bill and claim that it is reasonable.

There are further restrictions on service charges relating to major works to a building or other premises – but not to the services provided – judged by their cost. Most works are covered provided they 'qualify'. This means the lease must state that the flat owner must contribute to their cost, whether they are to be carried out to the building in which the flat owner lives or any other building. A special preliminary procedure must be followed if the costs incurred in total, not merely those attributable to a single flat, exceed the prescribed amount. This is £50 multiplied by the number of flats in the building, with a minimum of £1,000.

This amount has not been increased since 1988 and there have been complaints that it is unduly low and that it creates difficulties in blocks, particularly local authority-owned tower blocks, where very few of the residents are leaseholders. For example, in a block of 100 flats only ten of which are occupied by leaseholders, the landlord would have to consult the leaseholders about works costing in total as little as £1,001 even though their share of the cost would be only about £10 each.

Local authority leaseholders

Many local authority leaseholders face problems over high repair and improvement charges or an inability to resell their home on the open market. The Government has published proposals to give local authorities in England a financial incentive to buy back ex-council flats and houses.

The required procedure to be followed depends on whether there is a recognised association representing the flat owners or not (see *Tenants' associations,* page 111).

IF THERE IS A RECOGNISED TENANTS' ASSOCIATION

1. The landlord gives the association's secretary a notice with a detailed specification of the

proposed works, allowing a reasonable period for the association to suggest the names of contractors who might be asked to provide estimates. The landlord need not accept any suggestions made by the association.

2. At least two estimates must be obtained. At least one of the estimates must be from a contractor wholly unconnected with the landlord. A copy of each is given to the association's secretary.

3. Each flat owner should then be sent a notice briefly describing the proposed works, summarising the estimates (or enclosing copies of the estimates themselves) and informing them that they can inspect and take copies of the detailed job specification and estimates. The notice should ask for comments to be sent to a specified address within a period of not less than one month. Unless the works are urgent, they cannot begin until the time given by the landlord for comments has run out. The landlord has to pay some attention to any comments made by the flat owners.

IF THERE IS NO RECOGNISED TENANTS' ASSOCIATION

1. At least two estimates must be obtained for the work. At least one must be from a contractor wholly unconnected with the landlord.

2. Each flat owner should then be sent a notice describing the proposed works, accompanied by copies of the estimates. The notice should ask for comments to be sent to a specified address within a period of not less than one month. As an alternative to sending each flat owner an individual notice, a notice and copy estimates may be displayed where all the flat owners are likely to see them.

3. The landlord must 'have regard' to any comments received. Unless the works are urgent, they cannot begin until the time given by the landlord for comments has run out.

The sanction for not complying with the preliminary procedure is severe. Any excess in the cost, above the prescribed amount, cannot to be taken into account when calculating the service charge. A court has discretion to dispense with all or any of the requirements if it is satisfied that the landlord acted reasonably. An example might be if repairs are needed to specialised equipment, such as a lift, and only the original manufacturer will maintain its products, so that obtaining a competitive estimate is impossible.

Example

The exterior of a block of flats needs redecorating. Without warning, the landlord sends in a subsidiary company to do the work, which is delayed. The landlord did not seek estimates or give notice. The work is not urgent as shown by the delay and the fact that it only involves redecoration. The contractor is not independent of the landlord. The flat owners are liable to pay only the greater of £1,000 or £50 per flat. If the work is of a poor standard, then the relevant costs may not be reasonable and might be reduced even below the greater of £1,000 or £50 per flat if it is reasonable to do so.

Reserve funds

The arrangements for funding the maintenance and repair of a block of flats may include building up a reserve or 'sinking' fund from contributions included in the annual service charge. The purpose is to ensure that money is available for major items of expenditure, without excessive fluctuations in the service charge from one year to the next. Items that could be a call on such a fund are exterior redecoration, or the replacement of boilers and lifts.

Under the 1987 Landlord and Tenant Act, a reserve fund must be held on 'trust' for the contributing flat owners. This applies to all service charges, but is most important in relation to reserve funds. If two or more flat owners are paying towards the same costs in service charges, then the sums paid must be held by the person who received them (for example, a landlord) in one or more automatic trust funds unless the landlord is a local authority or other social housing organisation such as a housing association. If a flat owner's lease states that the funds belong to the landlord, the Act overrides the lease unless the lease specifically set up a trust covering the funds before April 1989.

Trust funds have to be invested in a limited range of secure investments and any interest or other income accrued has to be paid into the trust account. The funds have to be held on trust for the flat owners as the beneficiaries to meet the cost of the works or services for which they are paid. If there is any money left over after the costs for which the funds are earmarked have been incurred, the balance belongs to the flat owners in proportion to the sums they contributed towards the service charges. If a flat owner sells their property and moves, they are not usually entitled to a share of the balance of the trust fund. A flat owner's contributions remain on trust for future leaseholders. Moreover, if at the time a lease ends there are no more flat owners contributing to the same costs, then the landlord gets the assets of the trust fund(s) unless the lease provides otherwise.

The main advantage of the trust fund arrangement is that if a landlord or a managing agent becomes insolvent, the funds cannot be used to pay their debts. If a landlord or an agent misappropriate the funds, the flat owners can take them to court for breach of trust.

Flat owners are entitled to be given accounts showing where the money has been invested, how much is being made from the investments and proof that the income has been ploughed back into the fund. Flat owners should also be entitled to see any documents supporting these accounts. In any event, leases should provide for this information to be given.

A landlord who sells their interest in the property to another landlord is apparently under no obligation to transfer the trust funds to the new landlord. Leases should, but may not, put a specific obligation on the old landlord to allow the new landlord to take over the funds. The law is also vague about what should happen to the trust funds if they cannot be used for works or services but the leases continue, for example, the building has burnt down and cannot be rebuilt. In this situation leases should, but again may not, provide for the funds to be distributed between the flat owners in proportion to the amounts they paid in.

In many blocks there is a fairly rapid turnover of residents as existing owners sell and new owners move in. The problem thus arises of how to share out more equitably the cost of expensive works over time. Reserve funds, properly managed, are a sensible and practical method of spreading the cost out more fairly between former and current flat owners. As long as the work or services covered are clearly spelled out and the safeguards mentioned above are observed, flat owners' funds should be safe.

Demands for payment

A written service charge demand must contain certain basic information if the amount demanded is to be lawfully payable (1987 Landlord and Tenant Act). It must state the name and address of the landlord. If that address is not in England or Wales, an address which is must be given for service on the landlord (see *Information about your landlord,* page 109).

There is a time limit for making service charge demands. Flat owners are not normally liable to pay any charge relating to costs incurred more than 18 months before they received the demand. They do have to pay if, during that period, their landlord sent them a notice saying that costs had been incurred and that a demand would be forthcoming (1985 Landlord and Tenant Act).

Challenging service charges

If you are considering challenging the amount of or a specific item in a service charge, it is usually best if all the flat owners act together, preferably through a recognised tenants' association (see *Tenants' associations,* page 117). It is also important to keep copies of all correspondence sent and received. Flat owners should keep a diary or record of services provided and not provided, if the basis of the complaint relates to the provision or the standard of a service or services rather than to the amount of the charge alone. The courts have decided that a landlord who contracts to provide a service should do so, even if the flat owner is in arrears.

Example

Suppose a group of flat owners have decided to claim that the charges for central heating are unreasonable because the system does not work properly. In such a case, it would be advisable to keep a daily record of the dates, and perhaps the internal air temperatures, during the relevant period, say October to March. All the flat owners, or at any rate a majority of them, should keep a record.

All complaints should be made in writing, dated and copies kept, to show that the landlord or the agent was made aware of any failure in the provision or the standard of the service.

The usual first stage is to exercise the right to obtain information or to request a management audit (see pages 45-48). If your landlord fails to comply, then it might be worth considering asking the police or your local authority to prosecute. It is unlikely that either will. You may have to start legal action yourself.

The second stage should be to try to negotiate a more reasonable figure with your landlord or agent, if it is apparent from the information supplied or discovered that the demand is unreasonable. At this stage it might be worth consulting an independent professional, perhaps to get a report prepared or an alternative estimate, although you should weigh the cost of such professional services against the amount under dispute.

If you are unable to reach full agreement with your landlord, the third stage is to decide whether to proceed further, bearing in mind the amount still under dispute and, if so, which route to take. There are three options:

1. An application to a Leasehold Valuation Tribunal under the 1996 Housing Act provisions.
2. If the lease provides for it, either a landlord or a flat owner can apply to an independent arbitrator, who acts in accordance with the procedures of the 1950 Arbitration Act. Some leases require that a surveyor chosen by the President of the Royal Institution of Chartered Surveyors should be the arbitrator. Both parties need to agree to arbitration and an arbitrator's decision, once made, is binding.

Leasehold Valuation Tribunals were given powers to resolve residential leasehold disputes in 1997. They can now determine the reasonableness of service charges, settle disputes relating to insurance (see *Insurance,* page 113) and make orders, if appropriate, appointing a manager (see *Appointment of a manager,* page 121). Tribunals provide an easily accessible, usually cheaper and less formal route to the resolution of service charge disputes than legal action in a court. Each Tribunal consists of three members – a lawyer, a surveyor and a lay person (often a second surveyor) – and is independent and impartial. A Tribunal's service charge jurisdiction includes whether:

> > the works or costs are reasonable,
> > the works or services are of a reasonable standard,
> > an amount paid in advance of work is reasonable.

An application to a Tribunal may be made by an individual flat owner, a recognised tenants' association or a landlord. Although Tribunals are not courts, applicants and respondents to a Tribunal hearing are advised to seek professional advice before proceeding, particularly if the case involves a technical or legal matter. No application to a Leasehold Valuation Tribunal may be made on any matter which has already been formally agreed by a flat owner or determined by a court or by arbitration. Appeals from a Leasehold Valuation Tribunal may be made to the Lands Tribunal on any issue. There is no automatic right of appeal. To appeal the permission of the Leasehold Valuation Tribunal or the Lands Tribunal itself must first be obtained. The current addresses of local Leasehold Valuation Tribunals are given at the end of the guide.

The main advantages of a Tribunal are its semi-formal nature and the fact that there are no costs involved, except for the initial fee, unlike in a court where costs can be high and uncertain. Another benefit is that in the past leaseholders were entitled to seek a court declaration that charges were unreasonable but only when they had received the bill. Now they can challenge charges when works are proposed.

An application to a Leasehold Valuation Tribunal is subject to a fee, currently set at a maximum of £500 per application. The fee usually varies according to the number of flats in the building. The fee is payable in two instalments and there are arrangements for it to be waived or reduced in certain circumstances. The fee is usually waived when the applicant, or the applicant's partner, is in receipt of a means-tested social security benefit such as income support or housing benefit. Further information about fees is available from your nearest Leasehold Valuation Tribunal office.

A county court retains the power to decide issues concerning the proper interpretation of the lease itself. This may, for example, include determining if a particular charge is outside the scope of the lease altogether.

It is inadvisable to stop paying the service charge altogether or simply to pay only that part of it which you consider reasonable. You should normally continue to pay for items which are not in dispute. Although landlords can no longer commence 'forfeiture' proceedings for non-payment of service charges if there is a dispute, they can still seek to recover a debt in other ways. Forfeiture can only be used in relation to service charges if the flat owner agrees that they owe the amount or the amount has been determined by a court or tribunal or fixed by an arbitrator (see Forfeiture, page 33).

If your landlord brings court proceedings for non-payment of some service charge and you have paid a reasonable sum, you will have a defence which you must file with the court on the form provided. It would also usually be advisable to ask the court to transfer the case to a Leasehold Valuation Tribunal. If a court finds against you, you will have to pay the outstanding sum plus your landlord's legal costs and your own solicitor's fees. If you are acting individually, then this may be risky unless you are receiving legal aid. If you are acting through a tenants' association, legal aid is not available. It is usually sensible to pick a 'lead' case – a case which is typical of the other flat owners' cases – and agree that all the other flat owners will help to pay that person's costs in the event that the landlord wins.

Example

In a recent case, an individual flat owner unhappy with the failure by her landlord to provide certain services – largely the cleaning of the common parts – withheld her service charge. The landlord sued and the flat owner was ordered to pay the amount due, less a small sum for the services not provided.

Payments in advance may be challenged if they are unreasonable. A properly managed reserve fund, to meet the eventual costs of the repair or replacement of major items such as lifts or roofs, may be a better method of running a block than having to face large bills irregularly. Management costs are sometimes assessed, whether in leases or not, at a fixed percentage – say at 10, 15 or 20 per cent, sometimes even more – of the service charge. It could be worth challenging high management costs as unreasonable. Although the courts have upheld percentages, they have made it clear that no general policy can be entertained that any specific percentage is reasonable.

If you are engaged in litigation with your landlord or if, for that matter, your landlord is engaged in litigation with someone else, you can apply to a court or Leasehold Valuation Tribunal for a declaration that your landlord cannot pass on their legal costs in service charges. It has been held to be unfair that, if leaseholders have been successful in court or tribunal action, they should subsequently have to meet their landlord's costs via service charges.

3 Buying your building under the 1993 Act

Introduction

It has always been possible for flat owners, either individually or collectively, to purchase the freehold of the building or block they live in, provided their landlord wished to sell. Just over one quarter of all flat owners in England already own part or all of their building freehold. Many landlords do not relish the duties expected of them; especially in return for what some regard as a meagre income. Many commercial developers of blocks of flats have no desire to retain an interest in or manage a property once the flats have been sold. Very often such developers solve this problem by granting very long leases and vesting the freehold reversion to those leases in a leaseholders' company (see Chapter 7). Sometimes people inherit the freehold of a residential block. Either way they have no wish to hang on to it.

But many owners of blocks of flats did or do not want to sell their freeholds. Some derive a considerable income from their leasehold properties. In 1967, Parliament gave the leaseholders of houses the right to buy their freehold. With regard to flats, the breakthrough finally occurred in 1987. This right was extended in 1993 when flat owners were given a right to buy the freehold of their block as a group – a process known as 'collective enfranchisement' – whether their landlord agreed or not. Under this legislation – the 1993 Leasehold Reform, Housing and Urban Development Act – flat owners were also given a right to have their lease extended (see Chapter 5). Some defects in the 1993 Act were subsequently rectified in the 1996 Housing Act.

The purpose of this most important change in English and Welsh housing law was to meet the two main perceived problems with long leases of flats. First, a lease is a 'wasting asset' and over time it becomes increasingly difficult to mortgage a leasehold flat, thus affecting the property market and population mobility. Second, not all landlords are good landlords. Some are difficult to contact, others fail to carry out their repairing and other obligations, and some attempt to over-charge for services. If flat owners can buy the freehold of their block, they can grant themselves new leases, solving the first problem, and run their own management services, solving the second.

The 1987 Landlord and Tenant Act had earlier given flat owners a more limited 'right of first refusal'. It requires a landlord who intends to sell their interest in a block of flats to first offer it to the block's residents (see Chapter 4). In addition, flat residents have a right to buy their landlord's interest compulsorily at any time if a property has been seriously mismanaged (see Chapter 6). Although in many respects the rights under the 1987 Act have been replaced by those of the 1993 Act, it remains on the statute book and, in some circumstances, purchase under it is possible when it is not available under the 1993 legislation. A purchase under the 1987 Act can also often be cheaper than one under the 1993 Act.

This chapter looks at:
> the benefits of buying your freehold
> purchase under the 'collective enfranchisement' provisions of the 1993 Leasehold Reform, Housing and Urban Development Act
> getting organised for purchase
> the likely costs of buying the freehold.

The benefits of buying your freehold

Why should flat owners go to the trouble and expense of buying their freehold? After all they will still have a lease to their flat after the process is completed. Nevertheless, there are a number of identifiable advantages, and some disadvantages, which owners should consider before coming to a decision. These include:
> After purchase, you will have the power to grant longer leases without having to pay a premium for the grant.
> If there are problems with your existing leases, you may be able collectively to vary the terms of the leases. There would be no need to go to court to do this.
> You can together decide what is a reasonable service charge and you will be in a better position to ensure that you get value for money.
> You can together choose to carry out improvements to the building or add new

       amenities such as parking areas or recreational facilities.

> You will be able to decide collectively whether or not to appoint managing agents and to replace them if you are unhappy with their performance.
> You may find that your flat increases in value.
> You may find that it is easier to sell your flat if you own a share in the freehold.

Potential benefits need to be balanced against a number of drawbacks:

> Purchase may prove to be costly, awkward and lengthy.
> Unless you employ managing agents, you may find that being a member of the purchaser company is a time-consuming business.
> If you become a director of the new company, you may sometimes have to make decisions which prove unpopular with your neighbours. For further information on leaseholder management companies, see Chapter 6.
> You might have to face directly some of the problems of leasehold property management – dealing with arrears, nuisance residents, 'cowboy' builders.

The impact of leasehold reform

In 1996 an early assessment of leasehold reform was made on behalf of the government. While only 4 per cent of leaseholders in the sample had progressed to enfranchisement using the formal procedures, 16 per cent had bought their freeholds informally. Another 14 per cent were still attempting to enfranchise. Most of the remainder were either still undecided whether to proceed, or had suspended their interest in enfranchisement altogether. Another 5 per cent had completed the lease extension process (see Chapter 5).

Which tenants qualify?

The right to enfranchise (and to extend a lease, see Chapter 5) is only given to certain flat owners known as 'qualifying tenants'. This means a flat owner must have a long lease and, in a few cases, also pay a low rent. A long lease is one that was originally granted for more than 21 years. A shorter lease may qualify as 'long' if it is renewable by the leaseholder. The low rent test was abolished for most leases over 35 years long by the 1996 Housing Act and will therefore only generally apply to leases originally granted for between 21 and 35 years.

To find out if your lease is at a low rent, use one of the following tests:

> if your lease was granted between April 1963 and March 1990, a rent that was in the first year of the lease no more than two-thirds of the rateable value of the property; or

> if your lease was granted before April 1963, when the threshold is two-thirds of the letting value at the start of the lease; or

> if the lease was granted after April 1990 (when domestic rates were abolished), when it is a ground rent of £1,000 a year or less in London or £250 or less elsewhere.

There are some exceptions. A flat owner cannot be a qualifying tenant if:

> the landlord is a charitable housing trust and the flat is provided by the charity as part of its charitable work; or

> they have a business lease.

Generally speaking, you do not have to live in your flat to be a qualifying tenant. There is a residency test for enfranchisement under the 1993 Act (see later) but a flat owner does not need to satisfy it to be a qualifying tenant. But there are two special rules which mean that some non-residents are not qualifying tenants despite owning flats on long leases and at low rents if necessary.

1. Flats subject to more than one long lease. There can be only one qualifying tenant per flat. This is not a problem for joint tenants who are regarded as being one qualifying tenant together. It applies where a flat has an intermediate landlord who is also a long leaseholder. In that case, the junior leaseholder, not the sub-landlord, is the qualifying tenant.

2. Persons owning several flats. Although a qualifying tenant does not have to be resident, for the purposes of enfranchisement no one can be a qualifying tenant of more than two flats in the same building. If someone owns more than two flats, they are not a qualifying tenant of any of them. They may still be a qualifying tenant for lease renewal (see Chapter 5) but not for enfranchisement.

These rules mean that landlords who are themselves long leaseholders cannot enfranchise.

Which properties?

A single flat is part of a larger building or block. Under the Act, it is the block that is enfranchised – there is no right to buy the freehold of an individual flat. Flat owners have to join together to force the sale of their freehold.

A building can be enfranchised if it contains at least two flats and is either detached or vertically divided from neighbouring buildings and structurally self-contained. No part of it must be built on top of or beneath any other property and it must be capable of being redeveloped on its own.

There are three tests of eligibility for buildings:

> Mainly long leasehold. At least two-thirds of the flats must be owned by qualifying tenants. In a building where two-thirds of the number of flats is not a whole number, the fraction involved has to be rounded up to find the qualifying threshold.
> Mainly residential. No more than 10 per cent of the floor space (apart from common parts such as stairs) can be in non-residential use. Non-residential use includes shops, offices, workshops and also garages/storage units unless they are intended for the use of flat owners. So a block of flats with shops taking up all of its ground floor will probably have to be at least ten storeys high to qualify.
> Small converted buildings with a resident freeholder. If a property was converted at some time – not a purpose built block of flats – and

contains four or fewer flats and the freeholder or an adult member of his immediate family has lived in one of them as their only or main home for the last 12 months, it is not eligible for enfranchisement. This rule does not apply if the resident landlord is a leaseholder rather than the freeholder.

'Flat' includes a maisonette and properties which do not satisfy certain rules of the 1967 Leasehold Reform Act – the Act which gave the leaseholders of houses the right to buy their freehold.

Property exemptions under the Act are rare. The main exemptions are:

> Crown property is exempt although generally the Crown authorities permit enfranchisement and lease extensions (see Chapter 5) as if the Act applied to it.
> Certain heritage properties such as properties owned by the National Trust are exempt from both enfranchisement and lease extensions (see Chapter 5).
> Some private properties that have special tax status because they are open to the public are exempt from enfranchisement but not lease extensions (see Chapter 5).
> Properties in cathedral closes are exempt from both enfranchisement and lease extensions (see Chapter 5).

Additional requirements

Once it is established that a building is eligible for enfranchisement, there are three more tests to be satisfied.

> The two-thirds majority test. At least two-thirds of the qualifying tenants in a block must agree to buy the freehold and sign the necessary document. This rule is not affected by the presence of rental or commercial tenants in the building; so long as the building is eligible for enfranchisement, only two-thirds of the residential long leaseholders need support enfranchisement for it to go ahead but...

> The 50 per cent of flats test. The two-thirds majority of qualifying tenants must include the occupiers of a clear majority of all the flats in the building. Without this test it would have been possible in bigger blocks with a large number of non-qualifying tenants for enfranchisement to take place with the support of less than half of the occupiers.

Example

Take a block of 65 flats. Twenty are occupied by non-qualifying tenants; they are secure tenants of the local authority. Thirty one (69 per cent – more than the two thirds majority test) of the qualifying tenants support enfranchisement. But this is less than half of the occupiers of all the flats. The 50 per cent of flats test is not satisfied.

> The residency test. At least half of the qualifying tenants who agree to buy the freehold must have lived in their flats for at least the last year as their only or main home or, if not living there currently, they must have lived there for periods amounting to three years out of the last ten. They do not need to have actually owned the flat for the whole of this period. Companies which own flats, flat owners who have let their homes less than three years after moving in, and second home owners can still be qualifying tenants, but

enfranchisement can only proceed if an equal or greater number of other participants pass the residency test.

As before, fractions of whole numbers are rounded up. And as before this can have important implications for eligibility in small blocks.

Special rules operate in the case of blocks in which two-thirds or more of the long leases are due to expire within five years. The freeholder may be able to prevent enfranchisement if there are plans to redevelop the block. Flat owners whose leases are approaching this threshold need to act quickly to preserve their right to enfranchisement.

The process

If you and your neighbours wish to buy the freehold it is important that you obtain as much information as possible about the different types of leases, service charges, their lengths and the owners of the individual flats in your block. The following is an outline of the different stages involved and does not cover every detail of the enfranchisement process.

DISCOVERY NOTICE

It may not be possible to get all the information you need other than from your landlord. In that case, the Act allows the potential enfranchisees to serve a 'discovery' notice on the landlord or the managing agent requiring them to provide:

> the name and address of the freeholder and all those who hold other interests in the building including details of all the other leaseholders in the block; and

> details of those interests and any other relevant information.

The discovery notice does not commit you to buying the freehold. The landlord must supply the information requested within 28 days. A flat owner can serve a discovery notice on their own, so, at this stage, there is no need to get one's neighbours to agree to buy the freehold.

TENANTS' RESPONSE

Because enfranchisement is a group action, the other tenant(s) should be contacted at an early stage in order to decide whether to proceed or not. The rules for eligibility are complex and the first action should be to check that your building satisfies the rules and that there are sufficient qualifying tenants to be able to continue. You should make sure that:

1. Your building satisfies the rules:
   > Does it pass the 10 per cent commercial rule?
   > Are at least two-thirds of the flats let to qualifying tenants?
2. You and your neighbours make up the required number of participating tenants:
   > no less than two-thirds of the qualifying tenants
   > who own at least half of the total number of flats in the building
   > and half of the participating tenants must satisfy the residence test.

Example

There are 50 flats in a block. In order to enfranchise:

> The minimum number of flats owned by qualifying flat owners must be not less than two thirds of all flats – in this case a minimum of 34 flat owners.
> At least two thirds of these must support the application – in this case a minimum of 23 flat owners.
> But the participants in an enfranchisement application must represent at least half of the flats in the block – in this case 25 flat owners is the minimum number who must participate. Of these, at least one half must satisfy the residence test – in this case a minimum of 13 flat owners.

Before the process can proceed, there should be, if possible, a commitment from all those who have agreed to take part, otherwise qualifying tenants could drop out at the last minute. This commitment should, if possible, be legally binding on the participants: this is critical if the cost of enfranchisement is relatively high. This is much more important in smaller blocks than bigger ones because the financial implications of two tenants withdrawing from a group of ten are greater than two withdrawing from a group of 50. This is because their share of the costs will have to be spread out among fewer people.

You must prepare thoroughly before committing yourselves. At some point in the action, tenants will need to appoint a valuer and a solicitor. An initial valuation of the building is strongly advised so that you have an idea of the final purchase price before commencing the action. Once it is decided to buy the landlord's interest, you will need to agree who is to buy the property on the qualifying tenants' behalf. This 'person' is known as your nominee purchaser. You need to decide early on how you want your building to be owned and run in the future. Your decision will help you to choose a nominee purchaser. A nominee purchaser can be one of the flat owners or up to four as joint owners, a corporate body, a trust or a company. In most circumstances, especially in larger blocks, a tenant or leaseholder management company is the preferable format (see Chapter 7). A solicitor will be able to advise you on the mechanics of setting up an appropriate type of company.

It is possible to withdraw a notice to buy the freehold at any time before a contract is signed but you will have to pay your landlord's costs. If you withdraw, you cannot give notice to buy the freehold for another 12 months.

INITIAL NOTICE

Collective enfranchisement starts when the qualifying tenants, as a group, give 'initial' notice to the freeholder (known as the 'reversioner') and all other landlords. The service of an initial notice commits the qualifying tenants to paying the freeholder's and, where appropriate, the other landlords' reasonable costs. The notice must be given by not less than two-thirds of the qualifying tenants. The notice must:

> Give details of the freehold property which you want to buy. You may want the freeholder to give you certain rights over other property owned by them, for example, rights of way. If so, you must say what these rights are.

> Show the property affected on a plan, including the property you wish to buy.

> Say that, on the date you give notice, the building satisfies the rules for enfranchisement.

> Give details of any leasehold interests you want to buy, for example, a head lease. If the freeholder is a public sector landlord or a housing association, give details of any flats which must be leased back.

> Give the price you propose to pay for the freehold, for any extra property such as gardens, and for any leasehold interests. If the parties cannot agree, a Leasehold Valuation Tribunal can deal with disputes over the terms on which you buy the freehold, including the price.

> Give the full name and address of each of the qualifying tenants, including any who are not part of the group. You must include details of each qualifying tenant's lease and proof, if necessary, that each lease is at a low rent. You must also include details of how long those who satisfy the residence test have lived in their flats. These people must be at least half of the group.

> Give the full name and address of your nominee purchaser.

> Give a date, at least two months ahead, by which the freeholder must give their counter notice.

Once initial notice has been given, your landlord or someone acting on your landlord's behalf may visit a flat, at any reasonable time, to value the landlord's interest. Your landlord must give ten days notice before doing this. If a landlord had agreed to sell the freehold before the initial notice was served, and the flat owners were on the point of deciding to enfranchise, they have a choice. They can either exercise their 'right of first refusal' under the 1987 Act (see Chapter 4) or proceed with the 1993 Act's provisions. It may be more straightforward to purchase under the 1987 Act, but professional advice should be obtained first.

COUNTER NOTICE

The 'reversioner' must give a 'counter' notice to the nominee purchaser by the date given in the initial notice. In the counter notice, the reversioner must:

> agree there is a right to enfranchise and either accept the terms or suggest different terms. If there are any flats or other property within the

building which the freeholder has the right to leaseback and wants to do so, these must be mentioned. If the freeholder does not wish to leaseback any or all of this property, then the nominee purchaser will have to buy it. It is possible that an unwilling freeholder may try to obstruct your application by using this provision to increase the price you will have to pay. If the freeholder is a local authority or registered housing association, then they must take a leaseback of any flats which are occupied by secure or assured tenants. Advice on leaseback is essential; or

> give reasons for not agreeing that there is a right to enfranchise. You then have two months from the date of the counter notice to ask a court to decide whether the right to enfranchise applied when the initial notice was served. If you are successful, the court will order the service of a new counter notice. If you fail, the enfranchisement process is at an end; or

> say that an application to a court will be made for an order that the flat owners cannot enfranchise because they or one of the other landlords intends to redevelop all or most of the building. A landlord can only do this if at least two-thirds of all the residential long leases are due to expire within five years of the date the initial notice was served. The landlord must also show that, once the leases run out, substantial works to the building will be carried out which mean that vacant possession is needed. This is likely to be infrequent because the great majority of leases are likely to have many more than five years to run.

AGREEING TERMS

The nominee purchaser and the reversioner are allowed time to agree terms for the purchase of the property. The parties must enter into a binding contract within two months of the date when terms are agreed. If terms cannot be agreed, either party may refer the dispute to a local Leasehold Valuation Tribunal. If a reversioner does not comply with a time limit, flat owners may apply to a county court to order them to do so.

What about parts of the building not let to qualifying tenants?

Under collective enfranchisement, you buy the freehold of your block or building. You do not have the right to buy the leases of the flats or other units in the building which are not let to qualifying tenants. This includes shops, offices and flats let on short leases. The freeholder must take a leaseback of certain flats and can choose to do so in other cases.

If your freeholder is a public sector landlord, such as a local authority, it must take a leaseback of the flats it lets directly to secure tenants. If your freeholder is a registered social landlord (as are most housing associations) and has let a flat to someone other than a secure or qualifying tenant, it must also take a leaseback of that flat. Leaseback means a lease of 999 years at a peppercorn rent (a nominal rent which is not intended to be paid). If such leasebacks are taken, the price paid for the freehold will be reduced by the value of the leasebacks.

Any other freeholder may choose to take a leaseback of the flats or units not let to qualifying tenants. If your landlord decides not to take a leaseback of some or all of such flats or units, the nominee purchaser will have buy them and prepare to be the new landlord of the shops or rented flats in the building after enfranchisement. Some landlords have used this provision to increase the costs of enfranchisement in the hope that it will cause the flat owners to withdraw from the purchase. Of course, you can always sell such leases subsequently.

TIMETABLE

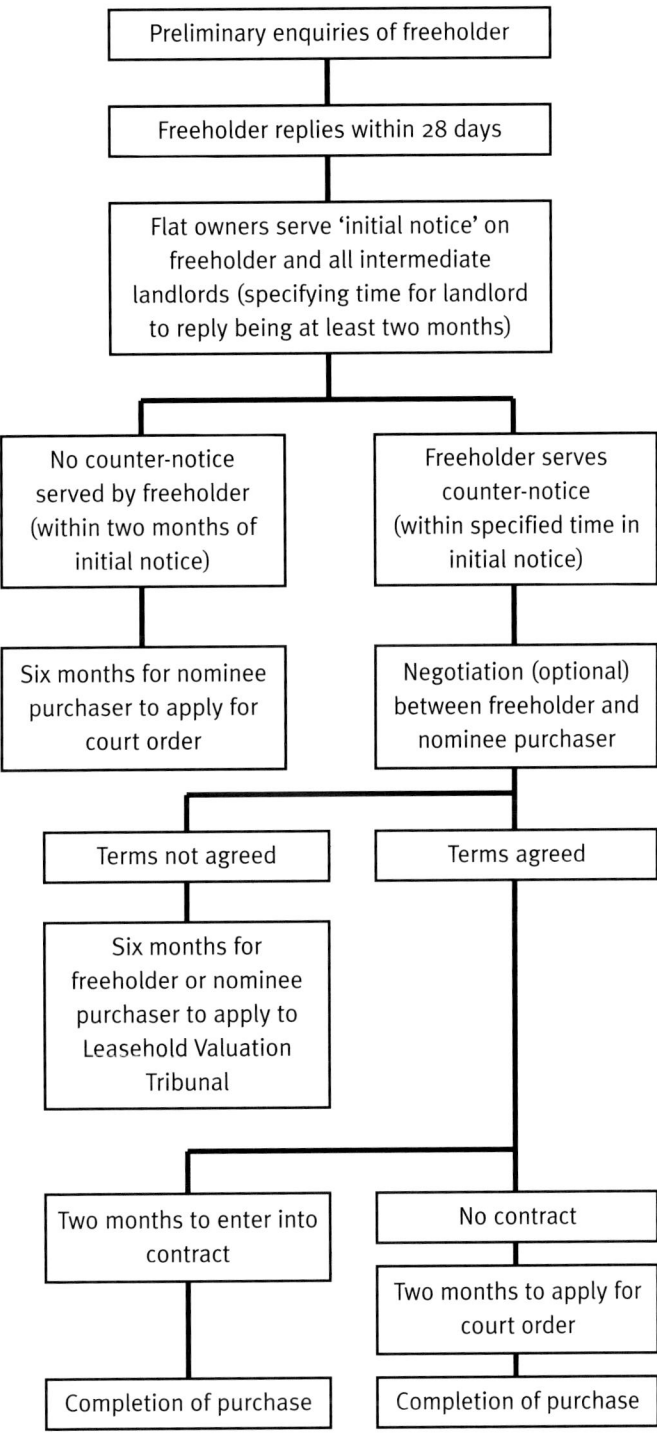

Preliminary enquiries of freeholder

Freeholder replies within 28 days

Flat owners serve 'initial notice' on freeholder and all intermediate landlords (specifying time for landlord to reply being at least two months)

No counter-notice served by freeholder (within two months of initial notice)

Freeholder serves counter-notice (within specified time in initial notice)

Six months for nominee purchaser to apply for court order

Negotiation (optional) between freeholder and nominee purchaser

Terms not agreed

Terms agreed

Six months for freeholder or nominee purchaser to apply to Leasehold Valuation Tribunal

Two months to enter into contract

No contract

Two months to apply for court order

Completion of purchase

Completion of purchase

Estate management schemes

Your building may be within the area of an estate management scheme. A scheme is set up in an area where properties are let by the same landlord who wishes to retain some powers of management over the properties. The aim is usually to ensure that the appearance and quality of an area as a whole is kept to the same standard. But a scheme can also provide for the upkeep of communal gardens or other common areas. Estate management schemes have to be approved by a Leasehold Valuation Tribunal. A scheme may:

> make provision for regulating the redevelopment, use or appearance of property;
> permit the landlord to maintain, repair or renew such property;
> impose obligations to maintain, repair or renew on those occupying such property; and
> permit inspections of the property.

If your building is covered by an estate management scheme, you can still go ahead with enfranchisement. But, after enfranchisement, your building will come under the rules of the scheme. If an application has been made for a scheme, you must wait until it has been approved, withdrawn or rejected. It does not matter whether the application is made before or after you give your initial notice.

Getting organised

A substantial amount of work needs to be done by or on behalf of the residents if the purchase of the freehold or the landlord's interest under either the 1993 Act or the 1987 Act procedures (see Chapter 4) is to be successful. Time pressure is usually not too significant, although an offer of the right of first refusal under the 1987 Act may come out of the blue. But there is a need to prepare thoroughly. In simple terms, the tasks that need to be undertaken include:

> checking eligibility
> organising for the purchase
> choosing and instructing professional advisers
> assessing the price
> establishing the finance and funding

> > dealing with the future management structure,
> > including selecting a nominee purchaser or
> > nominated person under the 1987 Act
> > gathering information
> > initial preparations
> > preparing for the subsequent process.

Each step need not necessarily be in this order and, in practice, several will run together. It is important, however, that each is carried out and that no significant issue is neglected. It is also essential that you commit yourselves to the process. In many cases, a clear and binding agreement between yourselves and the nominee purchaser/nominated person – to cover how you are going to share the cost of buying the freehold and meet the professional fees – should be entered into before you start the procedure. It should be remembered that each participant's flat will increase in value, sometimes substantially, particularly if extended leases are granted at peppercorn rents after the purchase has been completed. Once the initial notice or offer has been served, the process is up and running and you will be subject to demands for information and to deadlines. A default at any stage could endanger the process. At a certain stage in either of the two processes, you will become liable for your landlord's professional fees and costs. Nevertheless, the procedures are relatively simple, although cumbersome, and there is no reason why any group of tenants should not be able to successfully complete the purchase of the freehold of their block.

The costs

A decision about whether to buy the freehold of your block will often hinge on how much it will cost. Unfortunately, there is no easy way of arriving at a figure. Many purchases will take place on the basis of negotiation. The price paid will vary widely but is unlikely ever to be trivial. In some circumstances the cost may be substantial. This may happen if your flat is worth a great deal – especially true in many parts of London, if the leases are close to expiring or if there are non-residential premises, such as offices and shops, in the building and the landlord does not take a leaseback of them. And if the maximum possible number of residents do not participate, then those who do will have to pay proportionately more.

If you cannot agree a price with your landlord, the local Leasehold Valuation Tribunal can be asked by either party to determine one. In many cases, Tribunals are rejecting the high purchase prices put forward by landlords and fixing a price much closer to the leaseholders' valuation.

There is no precise formula for working out the price although the 1993 Act does set out a basis on which a price for enfranchisement (and for lease extensions, see Chapter 5) under it can be worked out. The price of the freehold includes three elements:

1. the open market value of the building which is, for enfranchisement, the value of the interests held by all the landlords in the property, assuming the flat owners are not in the market to buy; and
2. at least half the 'marriage value'; and
3. in some cases additional compensation to a freeholder for other losses. For example, the loss of development rights following transfer of the freehold.

The value of the interest(s) is, roughly speaking, what a third party would pay if the tenants stayed in the property. It reflects the value of the rents over the years left to run on the leases, the landlord's commissions (if any), and the value of the freehold. This if often a comparatively small sum, particularly if there are many years left to run on the lease.

Example

Take a 90 year leasehold flat worth £110,000. The landlord's freehold interest may be worth only £500 to a third party buyer. But once the freehold is bought, the property could be worth £125,000, giving a marriage value of £15,000. The flat owner will have to pay the freeholder half of this sum in addition.

'Marriage value' is the extra value created when the freehold and leasehold interests are combined and brought under the same control. These interests are often worth more together than apart and can often be the most substantial part of the price, particularly if all or most of the residential leases have only short or medium terms left to run before expiry.

The table on the next page indicates the total price that might be paid when purchasing the freehold of a block in which each flat is worth £100,000. It is intended as a guide only. It is apparent that the longer the lease, the less a leaseholder will have to pay. The figures shown can be used as a guide for a block of flats by multiplying the figure for each flat by the number of flats in the block. There are other parts of a block of flats that can add to the existing value, such as storage areas. The block may also contain units or flats which are not held on leases by flat owners who are qualifying tenants. If the freeholder decides not to take a leaseback of these properties, then the participants will have to purchase them which will consequently increase the cost of enfranchisement. The last component is in respect of other losses suffered by the freeholder as a result of having to sell the freehold. This may include redevelopment potential and increased running costs if other properties are owned by the freeholder and economies of scale are lost. But in most cases this will not be significant and will rarely be an item of claim at all.

The 'right of first refusal' procedure has no similar provisions to the above (see Chapter 4) which is why a purchase under it may be cheaper than one under the 1993 Act, because it does not include marriage value.

Illustrative example

Price payable per flat for different length leases for the purchase of the freehold

Years left on lease	Marriage value (£)	50% to freeholder (£)	+	Freehold value (£)	=	Payable to freeholder (£)
40	37,000	18,500	+	8,000	=	26,500
50	20,000	10,000	+	5,000	=	15,000
60	7,000	3,500	+	3,000	=	6,500
70	3,000	1,500	+	2,500	=	4,000
80	1,000	500	+	2,000	=	2,500
90	350	175	+	1,500	=	1,675

Assumptions

Example is based on a flat worth £100,000. £100 per annum ground rent. Interest rate 7 per cent. Freehold value includes value of ground rent income and value of reversion to freeholder. It is not practical to show the calculations involved in this illustrative example.

Examples

Two flat owners in North-West London with leases of 67 years bought the freehold of the property for a total of £67,650, a cost of £33,825 each. Six flat owners in Hounslow, West London, with 91 year leases bought the freehold of their block for a price of £7,075 each. It cost four flat owners in Cardiff £5,800 each to buy their freehold.

In addition to the cost of purchasing the freehold interest, flat owners will also have to pay their own and, usually, their landlord's professional fees – for solicitors, valuers and surveyors.

4 Buying your building under the 1987 Act

Introduction

Under the 1987 Landlord and Tenant Act, qualifying tenants were given the opportunity – the 'right of first refusal' – to collectively buy their landlord's interest in their building or block, but only if their landlord wanted to sell; and a right to require a new landlord to sell to them if the right of first refusal was ignored. This right was subsequently amended by both the 1988 Housing Act and the 1993 Act and was further strengthened by the 1996 Housing Act. In particular, it is now a criminal offence if a landlord fails to do what the law requires.

In addition to the right of first refusal, the 1987 Act also contains various provisions enabling certain tenants of flats to deal with bad management by their landlord. Part II of the Act entitles tenants to apply to a court for the appointment of a manager to take over their landlord's duties; while Part III gives tenants the right to acquire their landlord's interest compulsorily if their landlord is in serious breach of their management obligations (for information about both of these provisions, see Chapter 6).

Even if the residents do not wish to buy their landlord's interest, the Act's procedures allow them to delay the process for a minimum of four months without penalty. Such a delay may be sufficient to persuade a potential buyer, of whom the residents disapprove, to abandon the purchase.

The fundamental difference between 'collective enfranchisement' (see Chapter 3) and the 'right of first refusal' is that the first allows tenants to take the initiative, and permits them to buy the freehold compulsorily when they wish to do so. By contrast, the second leaves the initiative with their landlord. But if their landlord wishes to sell, which they are not obliged to do, they must offer the property to their tenants at the same price as they are seeking elsewhere. Another disadvantage of the 'right of first refusal' is that if what the tenants' immediate landlord has to sell is a lease, that is all the tenants will have the opportunity to buy. They do not have the right to buy the freehold if their landlord is not the freehold owner.

A purchase under the 'right of first refusal' is sometimes possible when it is not available under the 1993 Act. This is because more tenants are eligible and there are less severe restrictions relating to the existence of shops and offices in a building. In addition, a purchase under the 1987 Act can often be cheaper than one under the 1993 Act. The reason for this is that under the 1987 Act the price does not include marriage value (see Chapter 3). The other benefits and drawbacks of a purchase under the 'right of first refusal' are similar to those for 'collective enfranchisement' although it would not be possible in many cases for the new owners to grant themselves extended leases.

This chapter explores:

> The 'right of first refusal' under the 1987 Landlord and Tenant Act.
> The standard process and disposal by auction.
> How the right can be lost.
> What happens if the block is sold without the residents having first refusal.
> The principal differences between the 1987 and the 1993 Acts.

Which tenants qualify?

All tenants qualify for the right of first refusal, including long leaseholders and regulated tenants, except assured tenants, protected shorthold tenants and most business and service tenants. Flat owners are excluded if they own three or more flats in the building. A subtenant only qualifies if their landlord is not a qualifying tenant. Although more tenants qualify for the right of first refusal than for collective enfranchisement, it would often be a more effective and always a less expensive solution, especially if a large number of the residents of a particular block were tenants rather than flat owners, to pursue the option of applying to a court for the appointment of a manager (see Chapter 6).

Which properties?

The right of first refusal applies to the disposal of any property (not just a purpose-built block) containing two or more flats held by qualifying tenants, provided that more than 50 per cent of the flats in the property being sold are held by qualifying tenants.

If the building is used partly for non-residential purposes, such as shops or offices, flat owners and tenants will be excluded from the right of first refusal if more than 50 per cent of the floor space, disregarding common parts, is used for non-residential purposes.

Example

A building is made up of a ground floor shop and nine flats above. Two of the flats are vacant; six are owned by long leaseholders and one is let to a protected shorthold tenant. The six leaseholders are all qualifying tenants. As over 50 per cent of the flats are owned by qualifying tenants and as more than 50 per cent of the floor space is used for residential purposes, they have a right of first refusal if the landlord decides to sell the freehold.

In addition, buildings whose landlords are either local authorities, housing associations or other public sector landlords are excluded from the Act. A building which has a resident landlord is also excluded from the Act. A resident landlord is defined as a landlord who has lived in a flat in the building as their only or main home for at least a year at the time they wish to sell their interest in the property. However, a landlord does not count as a resident landlord if the building was originally constructed as a block of flats. There are special rules when there is a chain of landlords and the immediate landlord of the tenants of the flats has a leasehold interest of less than seven years, or there is an option allowing the superior landlord to terminate the lease within the first seven years. All other landlords are subject to the right of first refusal.

Which sales are affected?

Most sales or other transfers of a landlord's interest in a building – known as a 'relevant disposal' – are caught by the Act. Certain non-commercial transactions are allowed to go ahead without the flat owners and tenants being entitled to exercise the right of first refusal. These include gifts to members of a landlord's family, disposals to a charity, transfers to a landlord's heirs if the landlord dies, bankruptcy and transfers under a compulsory purchase order.

The right of first refusal does not apply if a landlord is selling the lease of a single flat in the building, or if the landlord is a company and it transfers its interest to another company within the same group of companies provided that company has been associated with the landlord for at least two years. It is probable that the right of first refusal does not arise if the landlord is a company and its interest in the property is indirectly sold by a purchaser buying shares in the company which owns the property rather than the property itself.

The standard process

If your landlord wishes to sell their interest in the property, they must first offer to sell it to the resident qualifying tenants. If your landlord enters into a contract with another landlord, before the first refusal procedure is started, then your landlord commits a criminal offence. The procedure is as follows:

LANDLORD'S OFFER TO SELL

Your landlord must serve a written notice which the Act calls a 'Section 5' or offer notice. It should include details of the interest being sold, the terms of the sale and the price, and offer to sell on those terms. This offer must remain open for acceptance for at least two months ('the acceptance period') and your landlord must allow a further period of at least two months for a person or persons to be chosen by the qualifying tenants to buy the landlord's interest on their behalf ('the nomination period').

The notice must be served on not less than 90 per cent of the qualifying tenants, or, if there are less than ten, on all but one of them. The fact that you might not have been served with the notice does not prevent you from joining the other qualifying tenants in accepting the offer or making a counter offer.

TENANTS' RESPONSE

If you are interested in buying your landlord's interest, or in delaying a sale, the other qualifying tenants should be contacted as soon as possible in order to discuss and decide what action to take. One possibility would be to call a meeting, perhaps of the tenants' association if there is one, to canvass views. Other residents must be contacted because a majority – over 50 per cent – of those qualifying for the right of first refusal must be in favour either of accepting the landlord's offer or of putting forward a counter offer for the process to proceed. If there are joint tenants or joint flat owners then they have one vote between them rather than one vote each. Swiftness in reaching a decision is important because the landlord may only have held the offer open for the minimum period of two months.

WHAT HAPPENS IF THE OFFER IS NOT ACCEPTED AND THERE IS NO COUNTER OFFER?

If a majority of qualifying tenants do not accept the landlord's offer or put forward a counter offer within the period allowed in the offer notice, your landlord is free to sell to whoever they like within the following 12 months without making a further offer. However, the sale must be on the same terms and at a price at least as high as that originally offered to you. If not, a criminal offence is committed.

WHO IS TO BUY THE PROPERTY?

If you accept an offer, you have a further period of at least two months from the end of the initial period to get organised. You will need to agree who is to buy the property on the participants' behalf. There must be a majority – more than 50 per cent – of qualifying tenants in favour of the particular person or persons concerned – known as the 'nominated person'. Each flat has one vote. The nominated person might be a company set up by the participants, one or more (up to four) individual tenants, an association or some third party. In most situations, a tenant or leaseholder company is the best option, as it is for collective enfranchisement under the 1993 Act (see Chapter 7). In effect, the nominated person will become the new landlord once the transaction has been completed.

SHOULD A COUNTER OFFER BE MADE?

If there are enough people interested in buying, you should always consider making a counter offer to your landlord's offer. This means asking the landlord to accept a lower price for their interest in the property than the price included in the offer notice. There are two reasons for this. First, if your landlord is anxious to sell without delay they may have no alternative but to sell to the qualifying tenants. The Act does not allow a landlord to sell to anyone else for a minimum period of two months from the date of their offer notice. A landlord might be prepared to accept a lower offer for the property to get the sale completed quickly.

Second, even if your landlord rejects the counter offer they will not be able to sell to a third party at a price lower than that in their offer notice. If you have reason to believe that your landlord's asking price is higher than the 'going rate' for their interest in the property then you should have the property professionally valued. If the valuation is lower than the offer price, you may be successful in persuading your landlord to accept it.

A Leasehold Valuation Tribunal has no power to deal with disputes over the terms on which a landlord's interest is bought under this procedure, including the price.

WHAT HAPPENS WHEN A COUNTER OFFER IS MADE?

If you make a counter offer your landlord can respond in one of three ways:

1. They can reject the counter offer without putting forward a fresh offer. In that case they will be free to sell to whoever they choose during the following 12 months without having to make a further offer to the qualifying tenants. However, the sale must be on the same terms and at a price at least as high as the offer to the qualifying tenants; or

2. They can reject the counter offer but continue negotiations by making a fresh offer to the qualifying tenants. If the negotiations are successful and a sale is agreed, the process will

continue in the same way as if the landlord's first offer had been accepted. If the negotiations break down, the position will be the same as if the landlord rejected the counter offer without putting forward a fresh offer; or

3. They can accept the counter offer. In this case, the process will continue in the same way as if the qualifying tenants had accepted the landlord's first offer.

HOW IS AN OFFER ACCEPTED OR A COUNTER OFFER MADE?

If a majority of qualifying tenants wish either to accept their landlord's offer or to make a counter offer they must serve a written notice to this effect within the period allowed by the landlord in the offer notice. The notice must specify the names of all the people accepting the offer or making the counter offer and the addresses of their flats. If a counter offer is being made, the notice must also set out the terms, including the price, on which the qualifying tenants are prepared to buy the property.

WHAT HAPPENS IF AN OFFER OR A COUNTER OFFER IS ACCEPTED?

Once a landlord's offer or the qualifying tenants' counter offer is accepted then, until the end of the period allowed by the landlord for a purchaser to be chosen (at least four months from when the offer notice was served), the landlord is not allowed to sell their interest to anyone except to the nominated person chosen by the qualifying tenants to buy the property on their behalf.

This period of restriction on a landlord's freedom to sell is extended by a further three months if a purchaser is actually selected by a majority of qualifying tenants within the time allowed by the landlord for a purchaser to be chosen.

If a purchaser is not chosen within the time allowed after agreeing a sale, a landlord is free to sell to whoever they like within the following 12 months without making a further offer to the qualifying tenants. The sale must be on the same terms and at a price at least as high as offered to the qualifying tenants.

WITHDRAWAL FROM THE SALE

The fact that a sale has been agreed by the acceptance of an offer or counter offer does not in itself commit the qualifying tenants or the landlord to proceed with the sale. This is because offers and counter offers are made 'subject to contract'; on the basis that no binding commitment to the sale has been made before a formal contract has been agreed. Once a formal contract has been agreed it will not usually be possible for one party to withdraw from the sale without the other's consent. Before this, either party can withdraw at any time.

THE LANDLORD WITHDRAWS

Withdrawal by a landlord will be in one of the following situations:

1. The property has ceased to be covered by the 1987 Act. This could happen if, for example, a flat in the building becomes vacant after the offer notice has been served causing the number of flats let to qualifying tenants to be less than half of the total number of flats. In this situation, a landlord can withdraw from the sale and will be free to sell their interest to whoever they choose without first giving the qualifying tenants an opportunity to buy. You should seek advice if your landlord claims this situation applies. Each party will have to pay its own legal fees in connection with the sale.

2. The property is still covered by the Act but a landlord withdraws prior to the qualifying tenants selecting a purchaser. In this situation, the landlord is not entitled to sell their interest in the property without making a fresh offer. Each party will have to pay its own legal fees in connection with the sale.

3. The property is still covered by the Act but a landlord withdraws after a purchaser has been selected but within three months of the passing of the deadline for choosing a purchaser. In this case, the landlord is not entitled to sell their interest in the property without making a fresh offer to the qualifying tenants. If the landlord

withdraws more than four weeks after the start of the period allowed for a purchaser to be selected, they will have to pay the purchaser's legal costs from the end of the four weeks to the time of withdrawal. Otherwise each party will have to pay its own legal fees in connection with the sale.

4. The property is still covered by the Act but a landlord withdraws after a purchaser has been selected but more than three months after the deadline for choosing a purchaser has passed. In this situation, the landlord is free to sell their interest to whoever they choose within the following 12 months. As before, the sale must be on the same terms and at a price at least as high as offered to the qualifying tenants. The landlord is entitled to their legal costs from the end of the four week period to the date of withdrawal. The person or persons chosen to be the purchaser together with the qualifying tenants who agreed to the sale will be 'jointly and severally' bound to pay the landlord's legal costs.

THE TENANTS WITHDRAW

This depends on when withdrawal takes place. Once a purchaser has been chosen, the qualifying tenants must withdraw by the nominated person serving a notice on the landlord to this effect. A withdrawal notice must be served if there is no longer a majority of qualifying tenants who wish to proceed with the purchase.

1. You withdraw after the offer or counter offer has been accepted but before choosing a purchaser. Before the deadline for choosing a purchaser, a landlord is not allowed to sell their interest without making a further offer. Once the deadline has passed, a landlord is free to sell to whoever they choose within the following 12 months. Again, the sale must be on the same terms and at a price at least as high as offered to the qualifying tenants. Each party will have to pay its own legal costs in connection with the sale.

2. You withdraw after choosing a purchaser. In this situation, a landlord is free to sell to whoever they choose within the following 12 months without

making a further offer. Again, the sale must be on the same terms and at a price at least as high as offered to the qualifying tenants. If the qualifying tenants withdraw more than four weeks after the start of the period allowed by the landlord for a purchaser to be chosen, then together with the person or persons chosen to be the purchaser they are 'jointly and severally' liable for the landlord's legal costs from the end of the four weeks to the time of withdrawal. Otherwise each side pays its own legal costs in connection with the sale.

Disposal by auction

This is a new procedure to allow landlords to obtain the market price for their property. It works by allowing the nominated person to take the place of the successful bidder at an auction. Again there are elaborate rules to be followed, similar in most respects to the standard process, although the time limits are often shorter. The nominated person has to accept the terms of the contract, including the price, and fulfil any conditions, such as to pay a deposit, agreed by the successful bidder at the auction.

Can the right of first refusal be lost?

The 1987 Act has a procedure under which a prospective purchaser of the landlord's interest can seek to ensure that the right of first refusal is lost. The prospective purchaser must first serve a notice on at least 80 per cent of the tenants of the premises they wish to buy which informs them of the terms and price of the proposed sale. The flat owners and tenants do not have to be qualifying tenants. The prospective purchaser's notice must invite the flat owner or tenant to serve a notice on them. This notice should ask whether the landlord has offered first refusal and, if the landlord has not, whether the flat owner or tenant knows of any reason why they might not be entitled to the right and whether they would like to exercise it. The prospective purchaser's notice must also warn the recipient how this procedure can lead to the right of first refusal being lost.

Unless at least 50 per cent of the flat owners and tenants served with the prospective purchaser's notice respond within two months then the right of first refusal is lost. It is also lost if more than 50 per cent of the flat owners and tenants served do respond within the time limit but they all say either that they do not think they are entitled to the right or they do not wish to exercise it.

Once the right of first refusal has been lost in this way, the prospective purchaser may safely buy the landlord's interest without first having to wait for the landlord to go through the process of offering their interest to the qualifying tenants. The purchaser also avoids the risk of the qualifying tenants subsequently pointing to a failure by the landlord to comply with the procedures laid down by the Act.

If you receive a notice from a prospective purchaser you should contact the other residents without delay and discuss what they intend to do. If the prospective purchaser is told that you wish to exercise your right of first refusal this does not commit you in any way. The next step would be for your landlord to serve offer notices on the qualifying tenants under the standard first refusal procedure.

What happens if the property is sold without the residents having first refusal?

If your landlord sells their interest in your block to a new landlord without first offering it to you, the new landlord can be ordered to re-sell it to you. If the requisite majority of residents discover that the property has been sold without their having had an opportunity to buy it, they can ask the new landlord for information about the terms of the sale. This is important because in some circumstances the new landlord is entitled to receive the same amount that they paid the old landlord. You will usually discover that the property has been sold when the new owner informs you of their name and address. Failure to do this is a criminal offence. If you have not been told the name and address of your new landlord, you have certain rights to obtain this information (see Chapter 6).

You have four months from the discovery of the sale to serve a notice requesting the information about the terms of the sale. The new landlord has one month to reply. You can serve a 'purchase notice' on the new landlord within six months of their response or, if no notice is served requesting the information, within six months of your discovery of the sale. If your new landlord fails to sell to you, a court can order them to do so.

Residents have similar rights in respect of any subsequent disposals. Disputes about the terms and valuation in these circumstances can be referred to the local Leasehold Valuation Tribunal.

The principal differences between the 1987 and 1993 Acts

	First refusal	Collective enfranchisement
Length of tenancy	Can be short letting, unless assured or protected shorthold.	Must be long tenancy.
Resident landlords	Not affected if flat in a converted block, occupied as only or main residence for 12 months.	Same conditions, but only apply if block contains no more than four flats. A relative can occupy.
Public sector landlords	Crown, local authorities, most other public authorities, charitable housing trusts and housing associations are exempt.	Crown (may voluntarily agree), charitable housing trusts (if flat provided for charitable purposes) and National Trust are exempt.
Subletting	Subtenant of qualifying tenant has no right, even if also qualifying.	Tenant at end of a subletting chain has statutory right, even if their landlord would qualify.
Use	Does not apply if over 50 per cent of block has non-residential use.	Does not apply if over 10 per cent of block has non-residential use.
'Trigger'	Only on 'relevant disposal' by landlord.	No limit.

Derived from Trevor M. Aldridge, *Law of Flats*, Longman.

5   Extending your lease

Introduction

All leases come to an end sometime. A defining feature of a leasehold is that it is granted for a limited period. All leases, when drafted, set out the length of the term of years agreed and its starting date. The exact date of expiry, if not explicitly stated, can easily be determined. When the lease expires, the contractual relationship between landlord and flat owner ends. The lease terminates at the end of the period without either party having to do anything.

While a lease has many years to run, it will be easily saleable and the prospect of homelessness is a distant possibility for most flat owners. The problem emerges towards the end of a long lease when a flat owner must face the imminent likelihood of losing their home and perhaps an expensive claim for any dilapidation to put the flat back into good repair. Flats with only a short term left on the lease are hard to sell or, at least, hard to sell at a good price. Mortgage finance is difficult, sometimes impossible, to obtain when a lease has 30 years or less to run and a loan is unlikely to be advanced to carry out major repairs.

Although a flat owner may benefit from some statutory protection when their lease ends (see Chapter 1), and can usually remain in occupation, in most cases this is as an assured tenant with reduced security paying a market rent. This is not as good as a new long lease, of course, but it is better than being made homeless. An astute flat owner, towards the end of a long lease, may seek to negotiate a large capital sum as an incentive to leave the flat, which may be the only way a landlord can get vacant possession of the property.

An alternative is to exercise either of the rights – to purchase the freehold (known as 'collective enfranchisement') or to a lease extension – contained in the 1993 Leasehold Reform, Housing and Urban Development Act. Enfranchisement is only possible if a large enough group of flat owners act together to buy the freehold, so it may not be a practicable option (see Chapter 3). The right to a lease extension is an individual right. If you do not qualify under either of these provisions, you may be able to negotiate a new lease with your landlord from the vantage point of being in possession.

Flat owners are entitled to exercise their right to a lease extension provided they are 'qualifying tenants' and satisfy a residence test. There is no need to wait until the lease expires; a lease extension can be purchased at any time. The new lease adds another 90 years to the time left to run on the existing lease. The new lease will be at a 'peppercorn' rent, but the other terms of the new lease will be the same as the old.

This chapter looks at:
> the benefits of extending your lease
> the lease extension provisions of the 1993 Leasehold Reform, Housing and Urban Development Act
> getting organised for a lease extension
> the likely costs of a lease extension
> the links with collective enfranchisement.

Benefits of extending your lease

Why should a flat owner go to the trouble and expense of extending their lease? After all they will still have the same landlord, albeit with a longer lease to their flat, after the process is completed. There are a number of identifiable advantages, and some disadvantages, which you should consider before coming to a decision. These include:

> The right to a lease extension is an individual right – you do not have to act collectively with the other residents.
> Since a lease extension can be bought individually there are no rules about majorities to be satisfied. You do not have to concern yourself with your neighbours or whether they agree with you.
> There are fewer circumstances in which properties are exempt compared with a purchase of the freehold.
> There may be insufficient qualifying tenants in a block interested in collective enfranchisement.
> The administrative complexity of the collective enfranchisement process may discourage you – the lease renewal procedure is in many ways simpler.
> There is no need to form a leaseholder management company.
> You may find that your flat increases in value.

There appear to be no serious disadvantages to buying a lease extension, provided the price is right. However, it does not solve any management or similar problems because your landlord remains the same as before and you will have less freedom to run your block than a purchase of the freehold would bring.

Which tenants qualify?

To have these new rights you must be a 'qualifying tenant'. Generally the rules for a lease extension are similar to those for enfranchisement under the 1993 Act (see Chapter 3). You must have a long lease which must be at a low rent, if necessary. However, if you own more than two flats in the building, you are not excluded from a lease extension. A resident may be a qualifying tenant for a lease extension of any number of flats in the block.

Which properties?

On the purchase of a new lease, the only property concerned is the tenant's flat together with associated land or accommodation such as a garden or garage. The characteristics of the block are not relevant. The presence in the block of rented flats, commercial property or a resident landlord are all immaterial. There are few property exemptions. The main example is where the flat owner's immediate landlord is a charitable housing trust and the flat forms part of the accommodation provided by the trust in connection with its charitable purposes.

Additional requirements

The residency test for lease renewal is stricter than the similar requirement for enfranchisement. When you give notice to buy a new lease, you must have occupied your flat, as your only or main home, for:

> > the last three years; or
> > periods that add up to three years in the last ten.

You do not need to have been the owner of the flat for the whole of the period. If you own your lease with someone else, only one of you need pass this test. A company cannot 'live' in a flat, so it cannot pass the test. This means a company cannot have the right to a lease extension. If a lease is within five years of expiry, a landlord can object on the grounds that they wish to redevelop the property (see Chapter 3).

The process

The procedures leading to an extended lease are similar to those for collective enfranchisement (see Chapter 3). But, given that there are only two parties involved they are considerably simpler. Lease extension is much more likely to involve another landlord rather than the freeholder of the property if such a landlord's lease is long enough: it must be more than ninety years longer than the flat owner's. A flat owner acquires a new lease either from the freeholder, or if there is an intermediate lease, from the owner of that lease, provided it is long enough to grant a new long lease. For example, if a flat owner has a lease with a remaining term of 30 years, any intermediate landlord must have a term in excess of 120 years. This is because the new lease will be for a term of 90 years plus the number of years remaining on the existing lease.

Example

Freeholder

Landlord A
Intermediate landlord with 180 years remaining on lease

Landlord B
Intermediate landlord with 90 years remaining on lease

Flat owner
With 25 years remaining on lease

A flat owner exercising the right to buy a new lease cannot serve notice on Landlord B because they do not have a long enough lease to grant the flat owner a new lease of 115 years. The flat owner has to serve notice on Landlord A.

As with collective enfranchisement, a flat owner can, without obligation, serve a discovery notice on their landlord and find out exactly who owns the freehold, where their landlord is based and, if there are any intermediate leases, obtain information about these as well. Again there is no prior requirement to obtain a professional valuation, although if you are contemplating extending your lease you should consult a valuer early on to find out how much you might have to pay. Advice on the legal issues involved would also be advisable.

INITIAL NOTICE

The process for a lease extension is similar to that for enfranchisement (see Chapter 3). A flat owner who decides to buy a new lease must serve a formal notice on the landlord. The landlord must have a lease longer than the flat owner's by more than 90 years. If there is no such landlord, then the notice should be given to the freeholder.

There is no set form for the notice, but it must give:

> your full name and the address of your flat
> a description of your flat
> details of your lease
> evidence to show you are a qualifying tenant
> proof that you satisfy the residence test
> the price you propose to pay for the new lease
> full details if you think the new lease should have different terms to the old one
> the name of any agent acting for you
> a date, at least two months ahead, by which the landlord must respond
> details of other parties, if any, being served with the notice.

A copy of the notice should be sent to any other person who owns an intermediate lease above the flat owner's but below that of the landlord or freeholder to whom it is being given. Once notice has been given, your landlord or their agent may visit your flat at any reasonable time to value the landlord's interest. Ten days notice of such a visit must be given.

COUNTER NOTICE

Your landlord must give counter notice by the date specified in your notice. In it your landlord must:

> agree that you have a right to a new lease and either accept your terms or suggest different ones; or
> give reasons for not agreeing that you have the right to a new lease. You may, within two months of the date of the counter notice, ask a court to decide whether the right to a new lease applied when you gave your notice; or
> say if they will be applying to a court for an order that you may not have a new lease because they plan to redevelop all or most of the building. The same restrictions about this apply as to the enfranchisement process (see Chapter 3).

Situations in which a landlord can deny entitlement will be rare. If a landlord fails to respond to an application for a new lease, the flat owner has six months to apply to a court to have their proposals accepted. If a flat owner does not keep to the time limits, their application for lease renewal is treated as being withdrawn. They become liable for the landlord's reasonable costs and are prevented from making a fresh application for one year. A landlord is entitled at any time after receipt of the flat owner's notice to require the payment of a deposit. This may be 10 per cent of the premium proposed in the flat owner's notice or £250, whichever is the greater.

AGREEING TERMS

You have at least two months to negotiate with your landlord over the terms of the purchase. If you cannot agree, you may apply to the local Leasehold Valuation Tribunal for the terms, including the price, to be settled.

Assuming that a flat owner's entitlement to a new lease has been accepted and that any disputes over the terms or price have been resolved, then the landlord must grant a new lease.

The new lease will be for a term of 90 years plus the number of years remaining on the existing lease. No ground rent is payable for the entire lease term; it will be at a 'peppercorn'. The new lease's provisions will usually be the same as those of the existing lease. If new provisions are required or added (for example, to take account of any alterations to the flat or to remedy a defect in the lease), they will only take effect after the termination of the flat owner's existing lease, unless otherwise agreed.

After you have bought a new lease, your landlord has a new right to apply to a court in the future for possession of your flat for redevelopment purposes. Your landlord is only able to do this:

> during the 12 months before your old lease was going to run out; or
> during the five years before the date your new lease runs out.

This right is subject to the payment of full compensation for the market value of the lease.

Example

If an existing lease has 20 years to run and the flat owner obtains a new lease for 110 years, any new provisions will only take effect after 20 years, although no ground rent will be payable from the start of the new lease.

Getting organised

A substantial amount of work needs to be done by or on behalf of the flat owner if the purchase of a new lease is to be successful. This includes:

> checking eligibility
> choosing and instructing professional advisers
> assessing the premium
> establishing the finance
> gathering information
> initial preparations, including drawing up the notice
> preparing for the subsequent process.

Each step need not necessarily be in this order and, in practice, several will run together. It is important, however, that each is carried out and that no significant issue is neglected. Once the initial notice has been served, the process is up and running and you will be subject to demands for information and to deadlines. A default at any stage could endanger the process. After service of the notice, you will be liable for the landlord's professional fees and expenses, whether you complete or not. Nevertheless, the procedures are straightforward and there is no reason why you should not be able to successfully complete a lease extension application.

The costs

As with enfranchisement, a decision about obtaining a new lease will often hinge on the total costs involved. A flat owner has to pay a premium for the purchase of a new lease together with the landlord's professional costs, including solicitor's and surveyor's fees. A flat owner can obtain advice about valuation and valuers must assess the value of a new lease in accordance with the principles set out in the legislation. Valuation is not an exact science and it is almost impossible to calculate a single, fixed price. Usually, valuers provide a 'best' and a 'worst' figure so that a flat owner will know, in advance, the likely range within which the price will eventually be settled. As with enfranchisement, there is no precise formula for working out the price although the 1993 Act does set out a basis on which it can be worked out.

The price of a new lease includes three elements:

1. the open market value of the flat which is the reduction in the value of the landlord's interests in your flat affected by the grant of a new lease; and
2. at least half the 'marriage value'; and
3. in some cases, compensation to a landlord for other losses.

The value of the interest(s) is, roughly speaking, what a third party would pay if the tenants stayed in the property. It reflects the value of the rents over the years left to run on the leases, the landlord's commissions (if any), and the value of the freehold. This if often a comparatively small sum, particularly if there are many years left to run on the lease.

The value of a flat owner's interest increases when they buy a new lease while the value of the landlord's interest falls. But there will often be an overall increase in the total value of the two interests. The difference between the total value of the interests before and after lease renewal is the 'marriage value'. This is calculated differently than it is for collective enfranchisement.

Illustrative example

A lease has 60 years left to run and a ground rent of £100 a year is payable. The current value of the flat is £90,000 but with an additional 90 years lease it will be worth £99,000. The value to the flat owner will thus increase by £9,000. In this case, the landlord's interest will be reduced by about £3,000. The marriage value will be about £6,000. The landlord is entitled to at least half of this (£3,000). In this example, the flat owner will have to pay the landlord a total of about £6,000 plus compensation, if any, and the landlord's reasonable professional fees and other expenses. It is not practical to show the assumptions or calculations involved in this illustrative example.

Flat owners buying new leases may have to obtain either a mortgage or re-mortgage of their flat. The position of mortgage lenders is safeguarded under the legislation. Any existing mortgage on the flat will be converted into a mortgage on the new lease.

The links with enfranchisement

Flat owners can apply for a lease extension before, during or after enfranchisement. Obviously, there could be problems if some flat owners wish to enfranchise while others wish to purchase a lease extension. This can only be sorted out by the individuals concerned. The legislation gives procedural priority to enfranchisement. If you apply for a lease extension during enfranchisement, the application will be frozen until the enfranchisement process has ended.

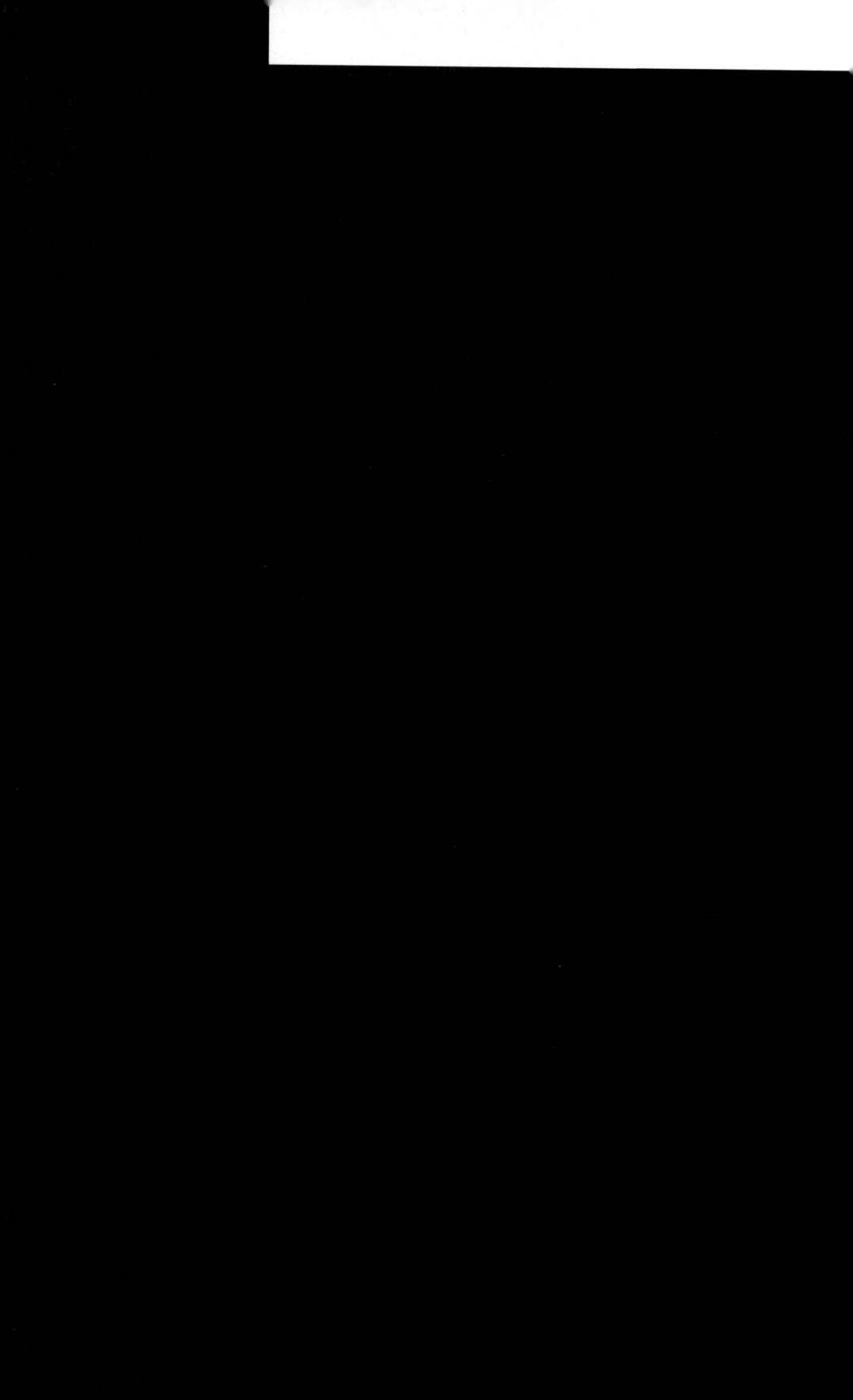

6 Other rights

Introduction

In addition to a flat owner's rights concerning service charges, to buy the freehold of their block collectively, to extend their lease and of first refusal, there are a number of other rights and duties. If a landlord does not follow these, there are various legal provisions available which may allow you to take them to a court or to a Leasehold Valuation Tribunal to enforce your rights. In some situations failure by a landlord to carry out a duty is a criminal offence for which a local council may prosecute.

The Secretary of State for the Environment, Transport and the Regions has the power to approve codes of practice governing residential property management. These are statements of the law or good practice and, if there is a dispute, the codes can be used as evidence of which management standards should apply. In addition, departure from the codes is now a ground for the appointment of a manager (see section on the appointment of a manager, page 121). The Secretary of State has so far approved only one code of direct relevance to blocks of flats. That is the Royal Institution of Chartered Surveyors' code covering properties where service charges are paid. A copy of this code is available from the Institution.

This chapter explains these main additional rights. They are:

> the right to information about your landlord
> the right to seek recognition of a tenants' association
> the right to information about insurance
> the right to be consulted about the appointment of a managing agent
> rights over repairs
> the right to seek the appointment of a manager
> the right of compulsory acquisition of the landlord's interest in the block

Your rights in connection with service charges, major works and management audits are dealt with in Chapter 2.

Information about your landlord

It has long been a concern that tenants should know who their landlord is. It is crucial to have this information, because most of the rights described elsewhere in this guide would be of little value in practice if your landlord cannot be identified or found. Various legal provisions – principally found in the 1985 and 1987 Landlord and Tenant Acts – have been introduced with limited success. The result has been further legislation, and the measures now overlap each over to some extent.

WHO IS YOUR LANDLORD?

The tenant of a flat has a right to know the identity of their landlord. A written request can be made to the person who demands the rent, or who last received it, or who acts as the landlord's agent. The recipient then has 21 days in which to supply a written statement giving the landlord's name and address. Failure to do so without good reason is a criminal offence.

If it appears that your landlord is a company, you can write again – to your landlord, the agent or the person who demands the rent – asking to be provided with the names and addresses of the company's directors and its secretary. It is an offence if, without reasonable excuse, your landlord does not give this information in writing within 21 days, or an agent or rent collector does not pass the request on to the landlord.

ADDRESS FOR SERVICE

By law landlords must notify flat owners of an address in England and Wales where notices can be served, for example, in connection with court proceedings. This may be the address of a representative such as a solicitor. If a landlord fails to do this, the flat owner's obligation to pay rent and service charge is suspended.

There is an exception to this rule if an independent receiver or manager has been appointed by a court (see later). In this case, the rent and service charge are due even if the demand does not contain the landlord's name and address.

If you do decide to withhold payment of the rent and service charge, it might be wise to pay the money withheld into your bank account to keep it on deposit until such time as the landlord provides you with the information.

CHANGE OF LANDLORD

When a landlord sells their interest in the property, the new landlord must inform the flat owners in writing that the sale has taken place and give their name and address. This information should be given within two months of the sale's completion or by the next day on which rent is due, whichever is the later. Failure to do so without good reason is a criminal offence. Furthermore, until the flat owner has been given this information, the old landlord remains liable for any breaches of covenant (for example, an obligation to keep the building in a good state of repair).

ABSENTEE OR MISSING LANDLORDS

Sometimes landlords cannot be traced. Their identity may be known but not their current address. Sometimes the name and address of a landlord is known, but they fail to respond. If the property is registered, a search can be made at the appropriate Land Registry office and the details obtained. This does not require the landlord's consent. You will need to complete a standard form for the purpose which can be obtained from legal stationers, some booksellers or from the Land Registry itself. The Land Registry in London will tell you where the appropriate office is for your area. Staff will be able to help you complete the form.

If your landlord's interest in the property has been sold recently, the Land Registry will not be able to give you the new landlord's name and address until the register has been changed. The address the Land Registry has may not be the landlord's current address because there is no obligation to notify changes of address. The Land Registry can refuse to give you the information if they think the owner of the property is not your landlord.

It is not unknown for landlords to vanish or to fail to respond to flat owners. This would mean that the landlord was in breach of their obligations to the flat owners. An application can be made to a Leasehold Valuation Tribunal to appoint another party, known as a manager, to act on behalf of the missing landlord (see section on the appointment of a manager, page 121). A majority of leaseholders can subsequently – after at least two years – apply to a court to acquire the building compulsorily (see section on compulsory acquisition, page 122). Alternatively, a court can appoint a 'receiver' to take over the landlord's duties. Similar rules apply when flat owners wish to enfranchise (see Chapter 3) or to extend their lease (see Chapter 5). Flat owners with absentee landlords will still have to pay the appropriate price for the freehold or the new lease.

An alternative option would for the flat owners to agree to undertake some or all of the landlord's responsibilities (for example, repairing the building, collecting the service charges, insuring the property, etc). But this may not be an ideal long-term solution.

Tenants' associations

Flat owners who have bought the freehold of or their landlord's interest in their block collectively, who thus become the landlord themselves, will of necessity have formed some sort of association (see Chapter 7). This short section is directed at flat owners who still have a traditional landlord.

This guide describes the legal rights and duties of landlords and flat owners. Some of these rights can be very effective. Others are less successful and should be strengthened. But it is almost always the case that the flat owners in a house or block can achieve far more if they act together through a tenants' association. A tenants' association can act as a 'watchdog' for the flat owners and for the other residents, if there are any. A landlord is more likely to take flat owners' views seriously if they are expressed as one voice. Although the legislation refers to tenants' associations, in situations where all or most of the residents of a block or number of blocks are flat owners, they may wish to call their body a 'residents' association' or conceivably a 'flat owners' association'. There are a number of organisations which can advise or help you set up a tenants' association including local private residents' federations, housing aid centres, law centres, local federations of private tenants. Some of these bodies have national headquarters. Relevant addresses are given in Chapter 12.

The 1985 and 1987 Landlord and Tenant Acts specifically
provide a role for recognised tenants' associations and
a method for an association to become recognised.
A recognised tenants' association can:

> ask for a summary of the costs for which you are
paying a service charge
> inspect accounts and receipts for the property
> ask to be sent a copy of the estimates, if
leaseholders are consulted about major works
> put forward names for the list of contractors to be
asked to tender for major works
> ask to be consulted about the appointment or
reappointment of a managing agent, and
> appoint a surveyor to advise on any matter
relating to service charges.

An individual flat owner does not have all of these rights.

An association must satisfy two requirements to qualify as a
recognised tenants' association. First, it must be an association
of qualifying tenants, that is tenants whose leases contain an
obligation to pay a service charge, with or without other
tenants. All flat owners will pay a service charge. A single
tenants' association can represent several blocks covered by
the same service charge arrangements.

Second, an association must be recognised. This can come
about in one of two ways. A landlord can give written notice of
recognition to the secretary of the association. There is no way
to compel a landlord to recognise the association.
If your tenants' association is refused recognition by your
landlord, the second way is to apply to your local Rent
Assessment Panel for a certificate of recognition. This will be
granted at their discretion. Usually the certificate will be for four
years, but the panel may cancel it if recognition is no longer
deemed appropriate. As a general guide, an association should
represent at least 60 per cent of the flat owners. The local Rent
Assessment Panel is found at the same address as the
Leasehold Valuation Tribunal (details are given in Chapter 13).

Insurance

Insurance is especially significant in a block of flats. Each flat owner and the landlord has a vital interest in the continuing upkeep and repair, indeed existence, of all the other parts of the building. Insurance of the building gives both the certainty and confidence that flat owners are ultimately protected from most eventualities including damage caused by fire, flood, subsidence, etc.

Contents insurance

It is obviously desirable for a flat owner to insure their belongings, furniture, fittings and decorations against loss caused by fire, flood, damage, burglary, etc. However, this will not be covered by the lease and is each flat owner's individual responsibility.

A single policy covering the whole building is the easiest way to ensure that a block is fully insured. The proper insurance cover is the full rebuilding cost, which may differ from the market value. Building costs are constantly rising, so the amount of cover should be regularly adjusted. This could involve a professional valuation but an inexpensive alternative is a policy which index links the sum insured.

If this is not done, a flat owner might be faced with a loss of thousands of pounds.

All long leases should expressly impose an insurance obligation. Since most blocks of flats are insured under a single policy, most leases make the landlord responsible for insurance of the building. Generally speaking the landlord takes out the insurance while the premium is the responsibility of the flat owners under the lease. Normally each flat owner will pay a share of the premium by way of a variable service charge to reimburse the landlord. If a long lease fails to make satisfactory provision for the insurance of the building and the parties to the lease cannot agree about how to amend it, either can apply to a court for an order varying the lease (see Chapter 1). Legislation, particularly the 1985 Landlord and Tenant Act, has given flat owners a right to information about insurance. These rights are additional to any provisions in the lease relating to information.

INFORMATION ABOUT INSURANCE

If the landlord is responsible for insurance, a flat owner or recognised tenants' association can ask the landlord or landlord's agent for a written summary of the current insurance cover. The landlord must provide this within one month. The summary should set out:

> the sum for which the property is insured
> the name of the insurer
> the risks covered in the policy.

Instead of supplying a summary, the landlord can supply a copy of the insurance policy itself.

Once you have seen the summary, or a copy of the policy, you have six months in which you can ask to inspect the insurance policy itself and any supporting documents, such as receipts, showing evidence of payment of premiums for the current period and for the period immediately preceding it. You are entitled to make copies of the policy and any supporting documents for a reasonable charge. The landlord must make the facility for inspection available free of charge for two months.

There are provisions covering information held by a superior landlord. In particular, if the whole or part of the information is needed from a superior landlord then the intermediate landlord is under a duty to go through a similar procedure to get it and the superior landlord is under a similar duty to provide it.

Failure without good reason to comply with these duties is a criminal offence.

UNSATISFACTORY INSURANCE ARRANGEMENTS

Leases sometimes specify that a particular insurance company must be used, but if not, whoever is responsible for arranging insurance cover is free to choose any company. Disputes often arise when a landlord chooses a more expensive policy which does not provide better cover than most alternatives. Sometimes this is because they get a commission from the insurance company. The cost of insurance must be reasonable. But the fact that cheaper insurance can be obtained does not necessarily mean you will be able to challenge your landlord's insurance arrangements successfully.

Example

In a recent case, the five leaseholders of a small block of flats were expected to pay £1,400 annually in building insurance. The Leasehold Valuation Tribunal ruled that they were being over-charged by their landlord and should be paying no more than £500 a year. They were also awarded backdated refunds.

Unless a lease states which company should be used, or what risks or perils should be covered, if the landlord is responsible for insurance all the flat owners can do is argue that it is unfair and unreasonable for them to have to pay the whole of their contribution towards the premium. The procedure is the same as that adopted when challenging another element of a service charge (see Chapter 2).

If the flat owner is responsible for insuring the property but the landlord has the right to nominate the insurer, there are special grounds for challenging the arrangement. These are:

> the insurance cover available from the nominated insurer is unsatisfactory in some way; or
> the premiums are excessive.

Such a challenge may be made to a court or Leasehold Valuation Tribunal which may require the landlord to appoint another insurer, or an insurer who meets specified requirements. The landlord's right under a lease to nominate an insurer cannot be removed and the landlord cannot be required to nominate a number of insurers from which the flat owner could choose.

NOTIFICATION TO INSURERS OF POSSIBLE CLAIM

A particular difficulty that sometimes arises when landlords are responsible for the insurance of the building is that they fail to claim promptly or fail to claim at all. Many insurance policies have strict time limits within which to make a claim. It is not possible for flat owners to make a formal claim unless they are party to the policy.

The 1987 Landlord and Tenant Act has come to the rescue of flat owners in this situation. You may write to the insurance company to tell them about a possible claim. You should also provide a brief description of the damage. This should be done within six months, or any longer period allowed by the policy. You should send the landlord a copy of the letter and remind them of their responsibility to make a prompt claim. If, despite this, the landlord still fails to claim and the insurance company refuses to pay, it may be possible to sue the landlord for damages.

Escape of water

One of the commonest causes of damage starting in one flat and damaging another is water, whether from damaged or defective plumbing or simply an overflowing bath. Comprehensive insurance policies, subject to the inevitable exclusions, usually cover the escape of water from tanks and pipes resulting from, for example, freezing or from defective heating systems. They rarely cover carelessness. The owner of a flat from which water escapes will often be liable for damages. It is possible to have an extension to a contents insurance policy to cover such an eventuality.

Managing agents

Landlords often employ managing agents to manage their property on their behalf. Problems can arise if a landlord appoints an incompetent, inefficient or dubious agent.

Example

The flat owners in a particular block pay an annual service charge of £800. Every time the managing agent of the block has, for example, a light bulb changed, a high charge is made but since receipts are provided, the agent is probably just on the right side of the law. The service charge in a similar block is around £300.

Often the best way to stop such practices is to change the agent. An individual flat owner has no right to be consulted about the appointment of a managing agent of their block. A recognised tenants' association may ask the landlord to consult the association about the appointment, or reappointment, of an agent. The procedure to be followed depends on whether at the time of the association's request there is already a managing agent or not.

NO MANAGING AGENT

Before appointing a managing agent the landlord has to serve the tenants' association with a notice stating:

> the proposed managing agent's name
> which of the landlord's obligations it is proposed the agent is to carry out.

The notice must allow the association at least one month to make comments on the proposed appointment and give the name and address of a person to whom the comments can be sent. Although a landlord has to take any comments into account, they can still go ahead and appoint the agent even if the association disagrees. The landlord has to follow this procedure each time there is a proposed change of agent.

EXISTING MANAGING AGENT

Within one month of receiving the association's notice, the landlord has to serve the association with a notice stating:

> which of the landlord's obligations the agent carries out.

The landlord must also give the association a reasonable period within which to comment on the performance of the agent and whether it feels the agent should continue to act in this capacity. Although a landlord has to take any comments into account, they can still retain the agent even if the association disagrees.

As long as the agent remains employed, the landlord should provide the association every five years with a notice specifying any changes in the landlord's obligations carried out by the agent. It must give the association a reasonable period in which to comment on the agent's performance since it was last consulted. As before, the landlord has to take these comments into account, but they are not bound by them.

If a landlord sells their interest in the property, the association loses its right to be consulted unless it serves a fresh notice on the new landlord requesting consultation.

If you are dissatisfied with the way the agent manages the property you should keep a diary or notes to back up your complaint. Complaints about an agent should be made in writing, the letters dated and copies kept. This provides evidence to support a demand that the landlord dismiss an unsatisfactory agent. Because a landlord cannot be forced to dismiss an agent and because it appears that there is no effective legal sanction against a landlord who completely ignores the consultation process, the most effective form of pressure to remove a poor agent is likely to be that mounted by all the flat owners acting together through a tenants' association.

Repairs

Even the most modern and well-built properties will deteriorate if left to themselves. To keep a building in satisfactory, let alone good, condition regular maintenance is needed. A building is a complex, interdependent structure: a fault in one of its parts can lead to more serious damage in another. Something as simple as a blocked gutter can lead to considerable damp penetration if it is left uncleared. Proper maintenance requires both time and money and can, in some cases, be very expensive. Unsurprisingly, therefore, the upkeep of a building is often neglected or avoided. Disputes about repairs are common. The law on repairs is complex, diverse and often incoherent.

If a flat is subject to a lease of more than seven years, a landlord is only legally obliged to carry out those repairs which are specified in the lease. The terms of the lease should set out responsibilities for the management, including the repair, of the building. For flats, the most common arrangement is that the freeholder or landlord is responsible for keeping the structure of the building, including the common parts, in good repair. The flat owner is normally responsible for the internal decoration and upkeep of their flat and for a proportion of the costs of repairs and maintenance. Flat owners will also generally have a responsibility to look after the property well.

If you think your building needs attention, you should first inform your landlord. You can write to the landlord and/or the landlord's agents requesting that they deal with each specific item of disrepair within a set period. The letters should be dated and copies kept. If you think something is seriously wrong, you can ask a surveyor to inspect the building and prepare a report setting out the details of the works which are necessary and send that to your landlord and/or the landlord's agent. It is sometimes possible to find a surveyor willing to prepare such a report without charge. If your landlord still takes no action, there are a number of different steps you can take. These are:

> Contact your local council. A council has broad statutory powers over the condition of housing. It has the power to serve a 'repair notice' on your landlord requiring that person to carry out specified repairs within a reasonable time. If a notice is not complied with, the authority can do the work and charge the cost to the defaulter. Failure to comply with a notice is an offence. The chief advantage of contacting a local authority is that it can take action against your landlord and you may not need to commence legal proceedings yourselves.

> Flat owners may carry out the repair themselves and deduct the cost from future rent (not the service charge). Before taking such action, your landlord must have had notice of the disrepair and the disrepair in question must be within the scope of your landlord's repairing obligations. This method is likely to be appropriate only when the repairs are relatively inexpensive given the modest sum paid by most flat owners in ground rent. It is not available to those flat owners who pay no ground rent.

> A flat owner's principal remedy against a landlord who fails to repair is to sue for damages and to seek a court order requiring that the work be done. Legal action of this sort should only be considered when the disrepair is serious and when all or most of the flat owners are prepared to act jointly. Compensatory damages can amount to thousands of pounds.
A landlord who does not comply with a court order may be liable for imprisonment for contempt of court. If the landlord is a company, the court may order a director of the company to be imprisoned.

> Some landlords may neglect their duties to such an extent that it is pointless for flat owners to take legal action against them over disrepair – for example, if a landlord has failed to carry out their

repairing obligations for a number of years or if the landlord cannot be traced. In such a case, a court may appoint a 'receiver' to take over a landlord's duties. An alternative is to apply to a Leasehold Valuation Tribunal for the appointment of a 'manager' if your landlord persistently fails to maintain a block consisting of two or more flats (see next section).

The owner of a block of flats is also liable in law for any injury or damage caused to an occupier of a property and to third parties, such as neighbours or visitors, by the condition of that property.

House renovation grants

If you own a property which needs repairs you may be able to get help from your local council to meet all or part of the cost of the work. The following are among the types of assistance available:

> House renovation grant – for the improvement and/or repair of houses and flats.
> Common parts grant – for the improvement and/or repair of the common parts of buildings containing one or more flats.

There are important qualifying conditions and each applicant is subject to a means test to determine eligibility for assistance. If you are in receipt of a means-tested benefit or on a very low income you could well qualify for help. If you are considering applying for a grant, you should contact the appropriate department of your local council before any work is started. Further details about renovation grants are available from your local council.

If you cannot obtain a house renovation grant to help with the cost of repairs or you need to make up the difference between a grant and the total repair bill, you may be able to get a loan or additional loan from your mortgage lender.

Appointment of a manager

If a building contains two or more flats, any flat owner can apply to a Leasehold Valuation Tribunal to appoint a manager to run the block or to carry out certain management functions under provisions in the 1987 Landlord and Tenant Act. The objective is to appoint someone to take the landlord's place to organise the work and collect payments for it.

Example

The leaseholders of a block of flats in Notting Hill, London won their application to appoint a manager of their choice at a Leasehold Valuation Tribunal hearing. The order removed all powers from the landlord who is now limited to receiving the ground rents. In addition to other poor or bad practices, the trigger was the landlord's behaviour over major works to the property. The owners were not sent estimates for the works – costing almost £7,000 per flat – and, since the works began almost immediately, had no opportunity to comment on the choice of contractor or the proposed works.

An individual flat owner may make the application but in many cases all or most of the flat owners may wish to act jointly. It is advisable to seek legal advice before embarking on this course. The grounds for seeking the appointment of a manager are:

> the landlord is in breach of their obligations to you as a leaseholder; or

> the landlord has demanded, or is likely to demand, unreasonable service charges; or

> the landlord has failed to comply with any relevant provision of a code of management practice approved by the Secretary of State.

Flat owners do not have this right if:

> their landlord is resident and you live in a converted building; or

> their landlord is a public body such as a local authority or a registered social landlord (most housing associations are registered social landlords); or

> the premises are included within the functional land of a charity.

THE PROCEDURE

A preliminary notice must first be served on your landlord inviting them to put right any problems if this is possible within a reasonable time. In certain circumstances, this requirement may be dispensed with. If your landlord does not put the problems right within a reasonable time, the next step is to apply for the appointment of a manager. The application should give the name and address of everyone likely to be affected by the application. It should also give the name, address and qualifications of the person the flat owners wish to act as manager. This is often a managing agent or a surveyor, but could be a company formed by the flat owners to manage the block on their behalf. In all cases a manager will only be appointed if it is just and convenient to do so.

Compulsory acquisition

As a last resort, again under provisions in the 1987 Landlord and Tenant Act, a majority of the flat owners in a block can ask a court (not a Leasehold Valuation Tribunal) to order the landlord to transfer their interest in the property to them. It is again advisable to seek legal advice before embarking on this course. The grounds for such a order are:

> the landlord is in breach of any obligation under the applicants' leases in relation to the repair, maintenance, insurance or management of the building and the breach is likely to continue; or

> an order for the appointment of a manager of the building has been in force for at least two years.

The first of these grounds is for use in extreme cases where the appointment of a manager would be an insufficient remedy.

This might be the case if, for example, the landlord cannot be traced. Again the building in question must contain two or more flats having the same landlord.

Flat owners do not have this right if:

> their landlord is resident and you live in a converted building; or
> their landlord is a public body such as a local authority or a registered social landlord (most housing associations are registered social landlords); or
> the premises are included within the functional land of a charity; or
> more than 50 per cent of the internal floor area of the building is used for non-residential purposes; or
> the total number of flats held by qualifying leaseholders is less than two-thirds of the total number of flats contained in the building.

A preliminary notice normally needs to be served on the landlord. An acquisition order cannot be made unless the court considers it appropriate to do so in the circumstances. The terms of the order are agreed between the landlord and the flat owners, or if they cannot agree, either party can refer them to a Leasehold Valuation Tribunal. The price is likely to be what the premises would fetch on the open market. The procedure for a compulsory acquisition is similar to that for the right of first refusal (see Chapter 4).

7 Leaseholder management companies

Introduction

More flat owners are buying the freehold, or their landlord's leasehold reversion, of their block collectively. This can be by voluntary sale, by 'collective enfranchisement' (see Chapter 3) or under the 'right of first refusal' (see Chapter 4). When the freehold or the lease of a block is bought, the flat owners will take over all the former landlord's rights and responsibilities. The question arises about how the landlord's former interest in the property should now be run by the flat owners. Usually the first step is to create a leaseholder management company whose role is both to hold a legal interest in the property and, more practically, to manage the block. Once a suitable leaseholder management company has been formed, flat owners need to consider such questions as organisation, meetings and managing agents.

Self-management by flat owners offers a number of advantages, including total control over maintenance and repairs, but requires motivation and effort to work effectively. In the early 1990s, it was found that in self-managed blocks, complaints by long leaseholders were only about one third and one fifth as frequent as where the landlord was, respectively, an individual or a property company. Although management companies can be an effective way for flat owners to gain control of their block, the system is still poorly understood by many residents and many professionals, and success is highly dependent on the ability and motivation of company members. Studies have found that there can be a problem of apathy among residents, especially in larger blocks.

There is not the space in this guide to examine all the aspects and implications of leaseholder management companies. The Federation of Private Residents' Associations publishes a useful guide, *Running a Block of Leasehold Flats,* which is obtainable direct from them (the Federation's address is in Chapter 12).

This chapter looks at:

> leaseholder companies
> organisation
> managing agents
> potential problems.

Leaseholder companies

You need to decide early on how you want your building to be managed in the future. What sort of body do you need to hold the reversion to the leases of the flats and to hold the freehold or take a lease of the common parts? Some forms of flat management can be informal. For example, perhaps the simplest form of management structure is the case of a building split into two or three flats. Responsibility for looking after the property can be shared equally between the owners and no other management structure is needed. The freehold may be vested in one or more of the flat owners. This sort of arrangement would be only practical or sensible in very small blocks. In larger developments, more formal systems for resident self-management are appropriate. The alternatives are to establish a trust or some form of corporate body such as an association or a company.

Other non-company alternatives for self-management

It is possible for two or more people to share ownership of a property with the relationship between them governed by a 'trust'. A trust consists of a number of trustees regulated by a trust deed for the benefit of specific beneficiaries. In a joint-ownership trust the trustees and beneficiaries are the same people. The trust deed would define each party's rights and obligations, including responsibility for common bills, maintenance and repairs. Trusts are governed by the Trustee Acts. A trust is not a corporate body: its income and liabilities are treated for tax and other purposes as belonging to the trustees. It is doubtful if a trust would be the most appropriate legal form for a group of more than six. A solicitor will be able to advise you about the mechanics of setting up a trust.

Another non-company alternative is to set up an independent legal association or society which registers as an Industrial and Provident Society. Its accounts have to be audited each year, and an annual report made to the Registrar of Friendly Societies who also has to approve the society's rules. Such associations are not strictly companies and do not operate under company law but must pool their resources on a self-help or co-operative basis. There should normally be at least seven people involved to form one of these. Members have limited liability for a society's debts. Individuals join or leave, but the corporate body lives on unless you collectively decide to dissolve it. Most housing associations are registered with the Registrar of Friendly Societies, from whom further information can be obtained.

In most circumstances, especially in larger blocks, a better choice is to set up a tenant or leaseholder management company which acts as a kind of co-operative or collective. This form of association allows the flat owners to be treated as a single body and, in addition, it provides a suitable degree of legal protection and a number of safeguards. Many developers of new blocks of flats create such companies because they have no wish to be responsible for management once the flats are sold.

Such companies can be known as a tenants', residents', owners' or leaseholders' management company or simply as a flat management company. Whatever their formal name, their role is both to hold a legal interest in the property and, more practically, to manage the block or building in which the flats are situated. They need to be distinguished from a tenants' association which, normally, does not have a legal interest in the property (see *Tenants' associations,* page 111).

A leaseholders' company will usually be incorporated as a company limited either by guarantee or as a private company limited by shares. There are advantages to both types depending on the circumstances and on the leaseholders' wishes. A solicitor will be able to advise you on the mechanics of setting up the most appropriate type of company. The liability of the shareholders or guarantors for the debts of a company is limited, usually, to the value of their share or their guarantee.

The company must comply with the Companies Acts, including registration with Companies House, have at least one director and a secretary and send a copy of its full or abbreviated accounts annually to the Registrar of Companies. The company must have a registered office which may be a flat within the block or elsewhere (for example, at your managing agents or solicitors). If the company hires staff, such as a caretaker, it must also comply with employment law. By law also the company becomes the landlord and will be subject to all the legal obligations imposed on landlords under current legislation. These include the right to:

> know how the service charge is made up
> inspect accounts and receipts
> challenge unreasonable service charges
> be consulted about major works.

Normally all the flat owners will be members or shareholders and they will be the only members or shareholders. To limit the members or shareholders to flat owners, a requirement can be inserted in the memorandum or articles of association to this effect. Putting the requirement in the memorandum, rather than the articles, renders it permanent and unalterable if the memorandum also prohibits any alteration of it. To ensure that all flat owners become members of the company, the normal solution is to include a condition to that effect in the lease.

Usually the board of directors of a leaseholder management company consists only of a number of flat owners. You may still need professional assistance, but co-operative management is likely to be better fostered if managing agents, auditors, etc, are employed by the company, rather than joining its board. An appropriate number of directors, including a company secretary, are chosen from among the flat owners and are subject to periodic re-election.

Depending on the situation, the freehold or leasehold reversion to the leases of the individual flats is vested in the leaseholder management company. Quite often, if it is a leasehold reversion, the leases are granted for 999 years – which to all intents and purposes makes it a 'freehold'. The freehold or a lease of the common parts is also usually granted to the leaseholder management company. Once the freehold of a block has been transferred to the new company, the leases of the flat owners can be extended, normally to 999 years. At the same time the opportunity can be taken to correct any defects in and/or vary the existing leases of the flats.

Organisation

Once a leaseholders' company has been set up properly, there is usually no need ever to concern oneself with its structure or objectives again. Experience shows that problems rarely arise with these aspects of a company. Flat owners do need, however, to concern themselves with the practical arrangements for running their block. Running a block of flats may seem a frightening prospect but many flat owners have managed it successfully. If there has been an effective tenants' or residents' association in the past, then you are likely to be familiar with much of what is involved. The chief difference will be that you will be commissioning work yourselves rather than checking on the actions of others.

Once the practical day-to-day arrangements are in place, running the organisation should be straightforward. These include:

> electing directors and a secretary
> arranging the annual general meeting of the company
> organising further regular meetings, usually on a quarterly basis
> budgeting for and setting of the service charge
> deciding whether to engage managing agents or not
> agreeing to maintenance contracts
> authorising and supervising major works
> dealing with employment of staff
> setting company policy
> preparing agendas for and minutes of meetings.

In practice, this work will depend on having sufficient flat owners who are prepared to do the work and to act as a director or the secretary of the company. Flat owners need to be encouraged to participate in the management of the block. Flat owners also need to report any defects in the property or their own flats and to suggest improvements either to the property or the management of the block. For example, it is perfectly possible for flat owners to decide to do some of the work previously carried out by paid contractors (for example, looking after the garden, decorating) although this should not be taken to extremes.

Example

The following is an example of poor practice by a leaseholder management company based in the Home Counties. In order to keep the service charge low, they decided that each leaseholder could do their own exterior work(!). Leaving such matters to individual leaseholders would thwart the purpose of collective management. It would be likely to lead to substandard work or the delaying of essential maintenance or repairs by some or perhaps most of the leaseholders – with consequent effects on the value of the flats. This is illustrated by the fact that the building's windows needed major repair or replacement but at least one leaseholder could not raise the money. Value is also affected if blocks of flats do not preserve a substantial degree of visual harmony.

In older blocks of flats, in particular, it is very important that timely maintenance and repairs are not overlooked.

Example

'In this block, the priority was to keep the service charge down. It was done at the expense of the fabric of the block. That went on so long that there just became a backlog of things that needed to be done. Hence the (major refurbishment project), and people are now having to pay for it.'

Resident director, London mansion block of 108 flats

The euphoria that can follow the acquisition of the freehold may soon disappear when the practical issues presented by self-management are realised. Self-management is not always a route to better management. Value for money services is a key benefit of self-management, but service charge arrears can be a problem, especially in larger blocks. There are reports of inadequate, even illegal, administration of leaseholder management companies. It is important that these questions are fully considered by flat owners. The most common stumbling blocks are more easily avoided if forward planning is undertaken. The national Federation of Private Residents' Associations can help. Run by a voluntary committee of lawyers, property professionals and leaseholders, the Federation is a non-profit making organisation which can advise flat owners before, during and after the purchase of the freehold (for its address, see Chapter 12).

Managing agents

In the vast majority of cases, it is preferable to employ a reputable managing agent to help with the day-to-day tasks of running a block. These tasks include:

> collecting the service charge
> paying bills, including insurance premiums
> planning maintenance
> obtaining estimates
> recovering debts
> paying wages.

The evidence is that management and maintenance planning tends to be better if a managing agent is employed. Most blocks of flats will already have a managing agent who used to act for the landlord. Unless you are very unhappy with their performance, it is better to retain them. You should choose a managing agent who is a member of a recognised professional body. A formal contract should be agreed between the company and the agent. The agent should agree to be bound by the appropriate professional code of conduct and to abide by the residential management code approved by the Secretary of State.

Potential problems

It would be untrue to pretend that a block which is resident-managed can be completely free of problems. Most of these will be similar to those which arose or might have arisen in the past. But dealing with owners who are in service charge arrears is comparatively straightforward compared with the distress and inconvenience which can be caused by anti-social or nuisance behaviour – excessive noise, inconsiderate residents or visitors, residents who damage the property or who fail to act in an appropriate manner. Unless it involves the block as a whole, it is best to leave neighbours to sort out things themselves. Excessive noise can lead to serious disputes. Local authorities and the police have powers to act if noise nuisance is serious. Ultimately, of course, it is possible to seek forfeiture, in reality a remedy for breach of the nuisance clause in the lease in such cases.

Problems are often caused by sub-letting. Most residential leases ban holiday-type and business lets but permit sub-letting. Many absentee landlords seem to lose interest in their property and its upkeep as long as the rent continues to be paid. Some also appear to believe that it becomes the responsibility of the resident flat owners to look after the premises and to 'police' their tenant(s).

Example

A flat in a small self-managed block of six flats in Essex was sublet by the owner to a succession of short-term tenants for over ten years. During this time the owner took no part in the management of the block, attended one residents' meeting and when a problem arose with her tenants, referred the resident leaseholders to her letting agent. Recognising that this was a breach of her obligations under the lease, the management company decided to ask her to contribute an extra sum to its service charge account. She agreed to this request.

Serious problems can arise if the subtenant(s) behave or treat the flat and/or the block in an unacceptable manner. The absentee owner should be contacted and supplied with the details. Should further action be necessary, evidence of the problem will be needed.

The Federation of Private Residents' Associations suggests that a set of 'house rules' for existing and new residents, including subtenants, be drawn up. These could be used to inform people about the arrangements for running the block – for example, dealing with maintenance issues or complaints, the disposal and collection of rubbish, postal deliveries, etc – and to remind them about their responsibilities under the lease – for example, to make service charge payments on time, to respect their neighbours' rights, etc. Such rules could be updated regularly if you wanted to highlight a particular issue.

Indifference by flat owners towards the management of the block can also lead to problems. Participating in the management of a resident-owned block is, of course, voluntary and you will find that many members do not attend regularly or, in some cases, not at all. Sometimes there are very good reasons, for example, health, family or work responsibilities. But sometimes there are not.

Example

'Some years ago we had a block of 104 flats... and the freeholder was going to hand it all over you know. They set up a meeting (and) six people turned up so that's your apathy... I've been to an AGM with those six committee members there, and one resident out of 104 flats. Why? Because they couldn't care less and a lot of them have sublet and are absentee landlords.'

Managing agent, large provincial town in the South-East

Apathy and complacency can be prevalent even in situations where, potentially, a large personal financial investment is at stake. One consequence of complacency is the risk that unscrupulous or dominating individuals may take charge of a management company and use it for corrupt purposes. You could point out that although participation is voluntary so is buying a property in a resident-managed block. A low participation rate is also likely to lead eventually to an increased service charge. It is difficult to suggest a permanent solution to this problem. If not enough flat owners are prepared to help in running the block, a greater workload will fall on a smaller number of people. As long as they are prepared to carry on and do not abuse their authority, few difficulties should arise. But if not, the whole arrangement could break down with potentially serious consequences for the future of the block. Making meetings less formal and furnishing an opportunity for general debate may boost participation and help generate a community spirit. Providing refreshments might encourage attendance and help people get to know each other.

Examples

One of the directors of a small leaseholder flat management company in Essex failed to attend a single board or general meeting, including the annual meetings, for nearly three years without explanation and never found the time even to discuss issues informally with the other directors. Consequently, the workload fell disproportionately on the other two directors. On average, less than 10 per cent of members attended quarterly meetings.

In a large block in central London, fewer than one in 20 flat owners attended regular meetings and the company found it increasingly difficult to fill vacancies for directors. In another large London block with over 200 flats, over the years an average of 12 owners took an active part in its management.

To the extent that indifference is the result of a lack of information provided to flat buyers, you could produce a 'welcome pack' for new residents telling them about the management company and its role. Copies of the pack could also be sent to a managing agent to supply to a prospective purchaser's solicitor or conveyancer.

8   Taking legal action

Introduction

Taking legal action is almost always expensive, time-consuming and worrying, and courts can often be unsettling and intimidating. Legal action should always be avoided if there are other ways of solving a problem or settling a dispute. You should first try to resolve a dispute by mutual agreement. If this is not successful, then you have a number of alternatives. This chapter briefly considers:

> Leasehold Valuation Tribunals
> arbitration and mediation
> legal action.

Leasehold Valuation Tribunals

Some issues – such as service charge disputes, the price of purchasing a freehold or the appointment of a manager – must now be taken to a Leasehold Valuation Tribunal rather than to a court to settle. Until recently, some of these could only be dealt with by a court. Leasehold Valuation Tribunals are more informal than court hearings, and it is not necessary, although it is often advisable, to be represented by a solicitor or other professional. Although there is normally an application fee, it can be remitted for those in receipt of most means-tested social security benefits or who have a civil legal aid certificate for cases transferred from a court. A Tribunal has the discretion to require any party to the proceedings to reimburse either part or all of the fee to the applicant. Unlike a court, it cannot award costs.

Arbitration and mediation

Other ways of settling disputes whilst avoiding legal action are to make use of arbitration or mediation services. Arbitration is a formal process involving an independent arbitrator, often a property professional, and is frequently specifically mentioned in a lease as a method of settling a dispute. Typically, arbitration is a method of resolving service charge disputes. Both parties need to agree to arbitration, there is a fee to be paid and an arbitrator's decision, once made, is binding on both parties. Mediation is a relatively new service set up by many voluntary organisations and local authorities around the country. The aim was to find a way of resolving, typically, neighbour disputes and the like, without resorting to legal action. Mediation is usually free and both parties need to agree to it in advance. Your local council should be able to put you in touch with the nearest mediation service. Mediation is probably not appropriate, and may not be possible, if you and your landlord are in dispute over an issue involving a large sum of money.

Legal action

Sometimes, however, legal action is the only way that a flat owner can enforce their rights, for example, to make their landlord carry out repairs. In such cases, it may be necessary to go to court to get an order to compel the landlord to carry out the repairs. On the other hand, if a landlord threatens legal proceedings and the flat owners have obtained legal advice that they have a strong defence, there may be no way of avoiding a court hearing.

The usual court in England and Wales for civil action about most leasehold issues is the county court. Criminal proceedings usually start in the magistrates court. You can find the address of those nearest to you in your local Yellow Pages, Thomson Local, etc.

Centuries of baffling legal terminology have been laid to rest in recent years. People bringing cases are now known as claimants not 'plaintiffs' while a 'writ' or 'summons' has become a claim form. New procedures have also been introduced in civil cases which provide for three tracks to deal with cases appropriately: a 'small claims' track is available for claims valued at not more than £5,000. A 'fast-track' is available for most cases valued at between £5,000 and £15,000. A 'multi-track' is available for more complex cases or those exceeding £15,000 in value. In some parts of the country, the government has launched pilot 'Community Legal Service' schemes to bring together the providers of legal and advice services into more co-ordinated networks. The aim is to provide a better service and better value for money. Civil legal aid is thought by the government to need radical change. A number of changes to the system, including the introduction of a strict 'funding code', have made legal aid harder to get in some cases.

If you are considering taking or defending legal action in a court:

> You should always get professional advice. You can get initial advice from Housing Advice Centres, Citizens' Advice Bureaux and similar consumer advice bodies. They are usually not able to give you expert advice on a leasehold problem but should be able to put you in touch with someone, probably a solicitor, who can. The Leasehold Advisory Service can provide advice by telephone, by letter or in person at its office but it cannot act directly for you, offer long-term supportive casework or provide any service usually provided by a solicitor or surveyor. Its address is given in Chapter 12. If court proceedings are approaching, your best bet is to seek the help of a solicitor. Ideally the solicitor should be one who specialises in acting for long leaseholders.

> Depending upon your income and savings, you may be eligible for civil legal aid or, as it is now known, public funding for representation. This means that your solicitor will represent you free of charge, or you will have to pay a monthly contribution from income or savings towards your legal costs. Public funding for representation is available for most court proceedings and Lands Tribunal hearings. A booklet about the current scheme for public funding for cases (the former legal aid scheme) is available from your local county or magistrates' court. If the legal action will benefit other people, for example, if you are seeking an order requiring your landlord to repair the roof of a block containing several other flats, then you might be refused legal aid or have to pay an increased contribution on the assumption that the other flat owners will help with the legal costs. In such circumstances, it may be necessary to select a 'lead' case – a typical case – and for all the flat owners to club together to pay that person's legal costs. If you win your case and you get or keep money with the help of legal aid, you may be asked to put it towards your legal costs. This is known as the 'statutory charge' and a leaflet explaining how it operates is available from the Legal Services Commission which now administers legal aid and public funding for cases. You may find a solicitor who will give you a free

interview or advice (up to a limit). The Law Society or a local Citizens Advice Bureau should be able to direct you appropriately.

> If you do not qualify for legal aid and cannot afford the full cost of taking or defending a legal action, some lawyers will take up your case without charging a fee. Your case has to be a strong one and most lawyers will want a share of any costs or damages awarded to you. This is known as a 'no-win, no-fee' arrangement.

> If you receive a court summons from your landlord, you must act very quickly. In some cases, you must file a defence within two weeks and, if you do not do so in time, you may be prevented from defending the case.

> If you lose a court case, it is probable that you will have to pay your landlord's legal fees as well as your own. Your opponent's fees are not covered by your legal aid. Such costs may run to thousands of pounds, particularly when the case has been a complex one, or if it has been dealt with in the High Court. If your case is heard in the county court, which deals with most cases involving claims for £50,000 or less, legal costs are still likely often to be in the order of thousands of pounds. However, cases involving claims for £5,000 or less will be heard as 'small claims' and the normal rule here is that each side just pays its own legal costs. In fast-track or multi-track cases (see above) the usual rule is that if you win, your legal costs will be paid by your losing opponent. However, you should remember that your potential liability for costs starts from the moment that a claim is issued and that, when deciding who should pay costs and how much, courts can even take into account conduct beforehand.

> If you think that you may become involved in legal action, keep all papers which may be useful and make notes immediately anything relevant happens (for example, a conversation with the managing agent or the date when you noticed that something needed repairing). If you make notes immediately after each incident, you will be able to use them to remind yourself when you are giving evidence in court.

9   Glossary

assignment

The sale of a tenant's lease to another person.

assured tenancy

A form of tenancy introduced by the 1988 Housing Act. Assured tenants have limited security of tenure and pay a market level of rent.

auditor

Usually a chartered accountant responsible for certifying that the accounts of an organisation are a correct and true representation of its financial affairs.

civil law

That part of the law which confers rights and impose duties on individuals and deals with resolving disputes between them. Most of the actions between landlord and flat owners are matters of civil law.

collective enfranchisement

This refers to the right of some flat owners to acquire the freehold of premises owned by the freeholder.

common law

That part of the law which is derived not from Acts of Parliament but from the principles and precedents set by earlier decisions of the courts

company

A corporate body registered under the Companies Acts. Companies are either owned by their shareholders or have members who guarantee to pay the debts of the company up to a limited amount.

contract

Any legally binding agreement.

County Court

The court which deals with the vast majority of civil cases in England and Wales, including landlord and tenant matters.

County Courts Act

Provides protection for tenants when a landlord is bringing proceedings to evict a tenant for non-payment of rent or service charges.

covenant
> An undertaking between landlord and tenant whereby they are bound to do certain things (such as to pay the rent or to repair); may be expressed (that is, set out in lease) or implied.

criminal law
> The part of the law which punishes behaviour harmful to the community as a whole, as against the civil law which confers rights and duties on individual people.

deed
> Written document which is sealed and which creates, varies or transfers legal rights or obligations, for example, which transfers property from one person to another.

demised premises
> Property which is the subject matter of a lease with certain implied covenants, such as promising that the tenant shall have quiet enjoyment of the premises.

easement
> A special kind of legal right which allows a property owner to use the facilities of another's land, for example, a right of way.

enfranchisement
> Tenant with a long lease buying the freehold of the property.

forfeiture
> The means by which a landlord can bring a lease to an early end following a breach of covenant by the tenant.

freehold
> The absolute ownership of property until the end of time as opposed to leasehold.

ground rent
> Small sum payable periodically to the landlord (the freeholder or ground owner) by a tenant who holds the leasehold property on a long lease.

implied
> Read into a lease rather than being spelled out in it.

landlord

The owner of property who grants a lease or sublease of the property (word is interchangeable with lessor).

Land Registry

A government department (head office in London and district registries in various other places in England and Wales) where details of properties with a registered title are recorded.

Lands Tribunal

Appeals from a Leasehold Valuation Tribunal can be made to the Lands Tribunal on any issue. There is no automatic right of appeal but only by leave of the Leasehold Valuation Tribunal or the Lands Tribunal itself.

lease extension

This refers to the right of some flat owners to seek a new lease.

leasehold

Ownership of property for a fixed number of years granted by a lease which sets out the obligations of the leaseholder, for example, regarding payment of service charges to the landlord, as opposed to freehold property where ownership is absolute.

Leasehold Valuation Tribunal

An independent local body whose members are drawn from a panel of valuers, lawyers and lay people. It deals with disputes over the terms on which a freehold or a new lease is bought, including the price. Since 1997, Leasehold Valuation Tribunals can determine the reasonableness of service charges, resolve disputes relating to insurance and make orders, if appropriate, appointing a manager. People who disagree with its decision can appeal to the Lands Tribunal.

lessee

The person to whom a lease was originally granted and, more commonly, the present leaseholder (word is interchangeable with tenant). In this book the term flat owner is used to describe a lessee, tenant or leaseholder who owns or is buying their flat.

lessor

The person who originally granted a lease; also, the present landlord.

managing agents

An individual or firm which manages a block of flats on behalf of the owner. Managing agents are usually chartered surveyors.

peppercorn rent

A nominal rent which is not intended to be paid.

possession claim (formerly possession action)

Exercising the powers or controls of ownership; procedure whereby a landlord goes to court to evict a tenant.

premium

Capital sum (the purchase price) paid for a long lease; also the payments to insurers for insurance cover.

protected and statutory tenancies

A protected tenancy is one that has security of tenure and rent regulation under the 1977 Rent Act. When a protected tenancy comes to an end by, for example, notice to quit, the tenant becomes a statutory tenant provided they reside in the premises.

Protection from Eviction Act

Law making it an offence for a landlord to evict a tenant without getting a court order.

qualifying tenant

A person who qualifies for collective enfranchisement or right of first refusal to buy the freehold of their home.

re-entry

Landlord lawfully retaking possession of a property with a court order on forfeiture.

register

In the case of a property with a registered title, the record for that property kept at the Land Registry, divided into the property, the proprietorship and the charges registers.

rent assessment panel

Locally based tribunal with a variety of functions including fixing rents, valuing properties and recognising tenants' associations. It is called a Leasehold Valuation Tribunal when it is dealing with issues specific to residential leases.

reversion

An interest in property which will eventually return to the original owner (or their successors) when the time during which another person holds the property comes to an end; loosely used to denote the freehold.

security of tenure

The right to remain in possession after the original contract has expired.

superior landlord

Someone with a higher interest than the tenant's immediate landlord. If A, a freeholder, grants a 99 year lease to B and then B grants a 21 year lease to C, the superior landlord is A.

tenant

The person to whom a lease is granted (word is interchangeable with lessee). In this book the term flat owner is used to describe a lessee or tenant who owns or is buying their flat.

term

This may mean either the length of the lease or a condition contained in the lease.

title

Ownership of a property.

valuer

A professional trained in property valuation. Most valuers are chartered surveyors.

10 Main Acts of Parliament

1954 Landlord and Tenant Act
1989 Local Government and Housing Act
> gives most long leaseholders the right to remain as a renting tenant at the end of their lease.

1985 Landlord and Tenant Act
> gives tenants, including long leaseholders, rights in relation to service charges
> consultation about major works
> right to information about and to challenge service charges
> rights relating to insurance
> recognised tenants' associations
> consultation about managing agents.

1987 Landlord and Tenant Act
> gives qualifying tenants, including long leaseholders, the Right of First Refusal
> appointment of a manager by a court
> compulsory purchase of a landlord's interest
> service charges to be held in trust
> variation of leases.

1993 Leasehold Reform, Housing and Urban Development Act
> gives most long leaseholders of flats the collective right to buy their freehold
> gives most long leaseholders of flats the individual right to extend their lease
> right to a management audit
> gives the Secretary of State power to approve management codes of practice.

1996 Housing Act
> makes it easier for long leaseholders to challenge unreasonable service charges and restricts a landlord's right to forfeit if an item or items of service charges are disputed
> strengthens the Right of First Refusal
> extends the rights of long leaseholders to buy the freehold of their building
> gives jurisdiction to Leasehold Valuation Tribunals to determine service charge disputes and applications for the appointment of a manager.

11 Useful publications

Please note that some of the publications mentioned below are aimed at law students and/or legal practitioners and are therefore often not accessible to the lay reader. If a book is mentioned, try to obtain the latest edition.

T. M. Aldridge, *Law of Flats,* Longman.

The College of Estate Management, *Flats As a Way of Life: Flat management companies in England and Wales, 1994.*

Government advice publications

Right of first refusal: for long leaseholders and other tenants in privately owned flats.

Leasehold flats: your right to buy the freehold of your building or renew your lease.

Long leaseholders: your rights and responsibilities.

Lease running out?: security of tenure for long leaseholders.

These are obtainable free from:

The Department of the Environment, Transport and the Regions
DETR Free Literature
PO Box No 236
Wetherby LS23 7NB

Tel: 0870 1226 236
Fax: 0870 1226 237
Text phone: 0870 1207 405
E-mail: detr@twoten.press.net

Companies House, *Flat Management and Similar Companies* (NG4).

Department of the Environment, Transport and the Regions, *Residential Leasehold Reform in England and Wales: A Consultation Paper,* November 1998.

Department of the Environment, Transport and the Regions, *An Analysis of Responses to 'Residential Leasehold Reform in England and Wales: A Consultation Paper',* Final Report, December 1999.

The Federation of Private Residents Associations, *Running a Block of Leasehold Flats.*

The Federation of Private Residents' Associations, *Buy-Outs under the Landlord and Tenant Act 1987 and the Leasehold Reform, Housing and Urban Development Act 1993.*

The Federation of Private Residents Associations, *Tenants' Collective Rights to Buy the Freehold and a Tenant's Individual Rights to Extend a Lease.*

The Federation of Private Residents Associations, *Participation Agreement for Collective Enfranchisement.*

The Federation of Private Residents Associations, *Summary of Rights.*

N. G. Fox, *Running a Flat Management Company,* The Royal Institution of Chartered Surveyors.

Leasehold Advisory Service (LEASE)

Collective Enfranchisement – getting started

Collective Enfranchisement – valuation

Participation Agreements

Leasehold Extension – getting started

Leasehold Extension – valuation

Application to the Leasehold Valuation Tribunal – valuations and terms of acquisitions

Application to the Leasehold Valuation Tribunal – service charges, insurance, the appointment of a manager

Appointment of a Surveyor/Management Audits

These are obtainable free from LEASE. Its address is given in Chapter 12. They are also available on LEASE's website.

Incorporated Society of Valuers and Auctioneers, *A Practical Guide to Residential Service Charges.*

Lord Chancellor, *Commonhold and Leasehold Reform: Draft Bill and Consultation Paper,* Cm 4843, The Stationery Office, August 2000.

The Royal Institution of Chartered Surveyors and the Chartered Institute of Housing, *Leasehold Reform, Housing and Urban Development Act 1993: A Guide to Part I and Part II,* 1994.

The Royal Institution of Chartered Surveyors, *Residential Management Code (Service Charge),* 1997.

S.J. Tabbush, *Resident-Owned Flats and Management of Freehold,* Sweet and Maxwell.

12 Useful addresses

Association of Residential Managing Agents
PO Box 1863
London
W10 4ZB
Tel: 020 8960 9077
Fax: 020 8960 9008

British Property Federation
7th Floor
1 Warwick Row
London
SW1E 5ER
Tel: 020 7828 0111
Fax: 020 7834 3442

Campaign for the Abolition of Residential Leaseholds
PO Box 3076
Littlehampton
West Sussex
BN17 5BT
Tel: 01903 856832
website: www.carl.org.uk

Companies House
Registrar of Companies
Companies House
Crown Way
Cardiff
CF14 3UZ
Tel: 029 2038 8588
Fax: 029 2038 0900
website: www.companies-house.gov.uk

London branch
21 Bloomsbury Street
London
WC1B 3XD
Tel: 029 2038 0801
Fax: 029 2038 0900

Council of Mortgage Lenders
3 Savile Row
London
W1X 1AF
Tel: 020 7437 0655
website: www.cml.org.uk

Department of the Environment, Transport and the Regions
– for England only
HPRS Division
Floor 2/F6
Eland House
Bressenden Place
London
SW1E 5DU
Tel: 020 7944 3462
website: www.detr.gov.uk

Federation of Private Residents' Associations
3rd Floor
Overseas House
19-23 Ironmonger Row
London
EC1V 3QN
Tel: 020 7490 7073
Fax: 020 7490 7074
e-mail: office@fpra.freeserve.co.uk

HM Land Registry (Headquarters)
32 Lincoln's Inn Fields
London
WC2A 3PH
Tel: 020 7917 8888
Fax: 020 7955 0110
website: www.landreg.gov.uk

Incorporated Society of Valuers and Auctioneers
3 Cadogan Gate
London
SW1X 0AS
Tel: 020 7235 2282

Lands Tribunal
48-49 Chancery Lane
London
WC2A 1JR
Tel: 020 7947 7200
Fax: 020 7947 7215

Law Centres Federation
Duchess House
18-19 Warren Street
London
W1P 5DB
Tel: 020 7387 8580

Law Society
113 Chancery Lane
London
WC2A 1PL
Tel: 020 7242 1222

Leasehold Advisory Service (LEASE)
8 Maddox Street
London W1R 9PN
Tel: 020 7493 3116
Fax: 020 7493 4318
e-mail info@lease-advice.org
website: www.lease-advice.org.uk

Leasehold Enfranchisement Ltd
33 St George's Drive
London
SW1V 4DG

Leaseholders Enfranchisement Association
26 Upper Phillimore Gardens
London W8 7HA
Tel: 020 7937 0866

Legal Services Commission
85 Gray's Inn Road
London WC1X 8TX
Tel: 020 7759 0000
Fax: 020 7759 0536
DX No. 328 London/Chancery Lane
website: www.legalservices.gov.uk

National Assembly for Wales
Housing, Performance and Finance Division
Ground Floor
Cathays Park
Cardiff
CF1 3NQ
Tel: 029 20 823025
website: www.wales.gov.uk

National Association of Citizens' Advice Bureaux
115-123 Pentonville Road
London
N1 9LZ
Tel: 020 7833 2181
website: www.nacab.org.uk

Registry of Friendly Societies
Victory House
30-34 Kingsway
London
WC2B 6ES
Tel: 020 7663 5276/020 7663 5274
Fax: 020 7269 9806

Royal Institution of Chartered Surveyors
12 Great George Street
Parliament Square
London
SW1P 3AD
Tel: 020 7222 7000
Fax: 020 7222 9430
website: www.rics.org.uk

Shelter
88 Old Street
London
EC1V 9HU
Tel: 020 7505 4699
e-mail: info@shelter.org.uk
website: www.shelter.org.uk

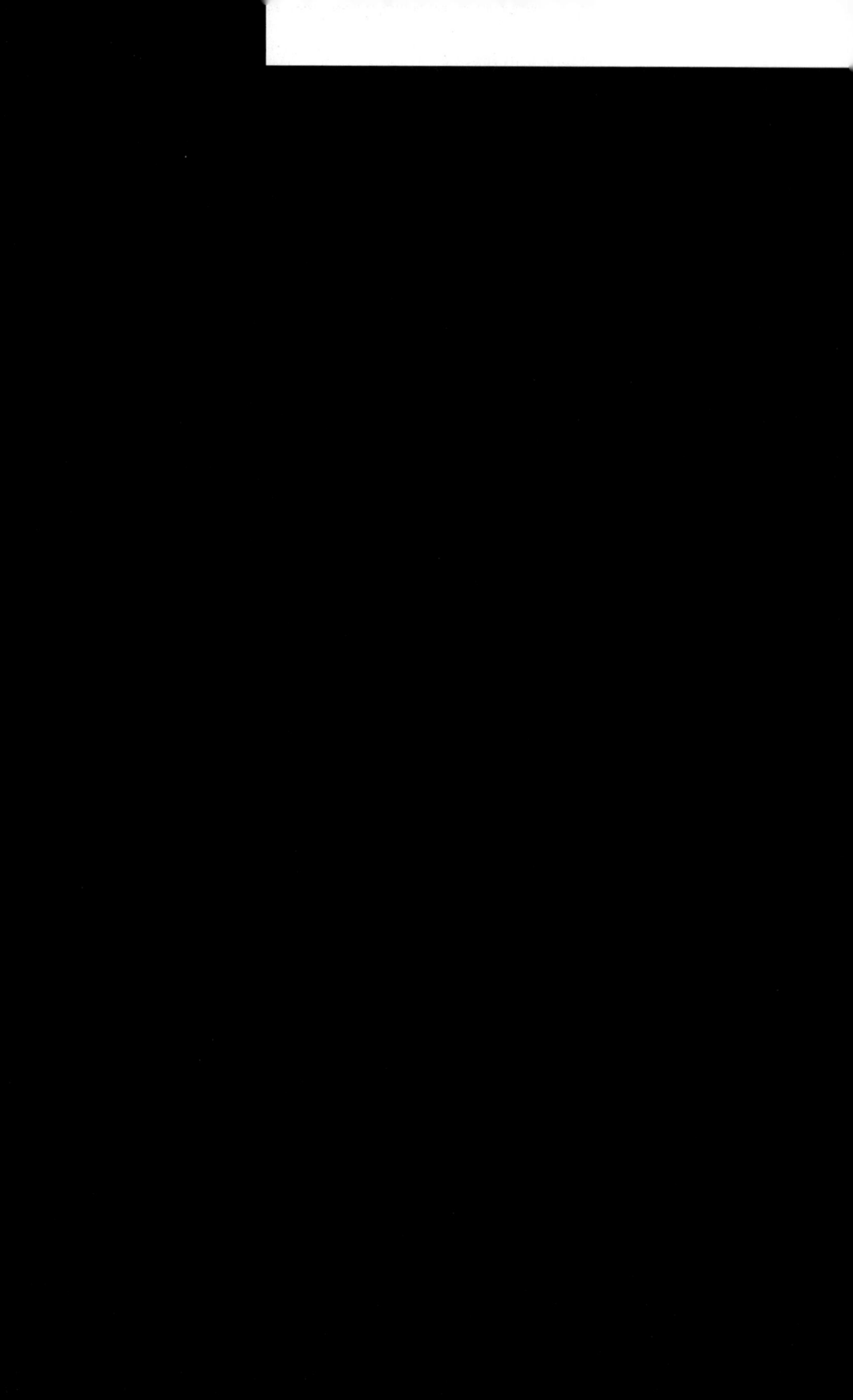

13 Leasehold Valuation Tribunals and Rent Assessment Panels

London
Whittington House
19-30 Alfred Place
London WC1E 7LR
020 7446 7700

Merseyside & Cheshire
Port of Liverpool Building
First Floor
Pier Head
Liverpool L3 1BY
0151 236 3521

North Western
20th Floor
Sunley Tower
Piccadilly Plaza
Manchester M1 4BE
0161 237 9491

Midlands
5th Floor
Somerset House
37 Temple Street
Birmingham B2 5DP
0121 643 8336

North Eastern
Warwick House
Grantham Road
Newcastle upon Tyne NE2 1QX
0191 201 3770

Symons House
Belgrave Street
Leeds LS2 8DD
0113 243 9744

Chilterns, Thames and Eastern
Great Eastern House
Tenison Road
Cambridge CB1 2TR
01223 505112

Southern and South Eastern

1st Floor
Midland House
1 Market Avenue
Chichester PO19 1PJ
01243 779394

South Western

Middlegate
Whitefriars
Lewins Mead
Bristol BS1 2AP
0117 929 9431

Wales

1st Floor, West Wing
Southgate House
Wood Street
Cardiff CF1 1EW
029 2023 1687

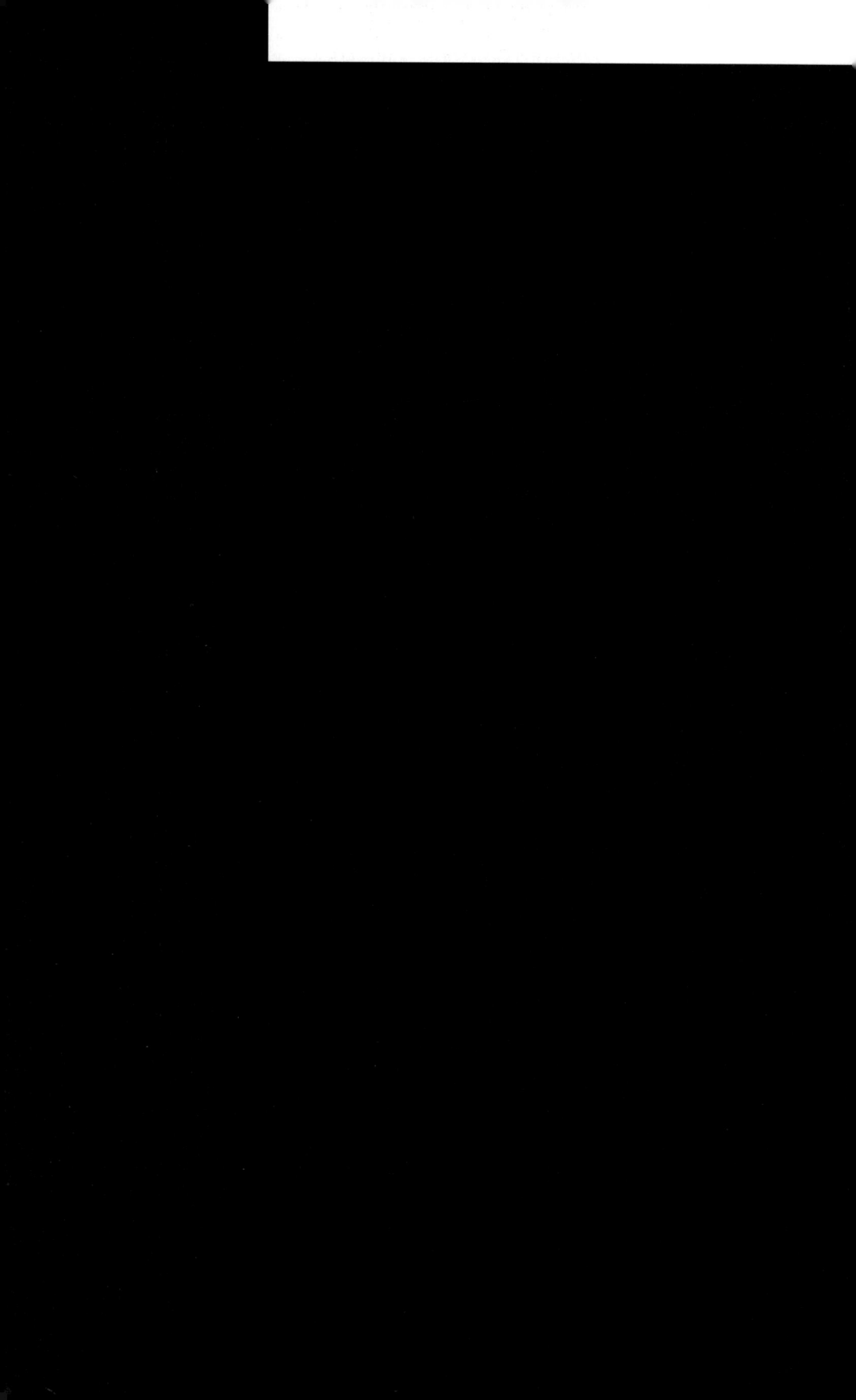

14 Index